"Dr. Mary Polce-Lynch mixes humanity and good science in discussing ways for people to write about life and death. There is solid evidence that writing about emotional upheavals in our lives can promote health. *Nothing Left Unsaid* takes this idea to an important new level, asking readers to contemplate their own deaths and imagine the impact on loved ones. By writing thoughtful good-byes, both the surviving loved ones and the writer can benefit extraordinarily. I'm very impressed with the power of this book and its potential to make a difference in people's lives."

—James W. Pennebaker, Professor of Psychology, University of Texas at Austin, author of *Opening Up*

"People die; relationships don't. Mary Polce-Lynch's profoundly moving book teaches all of us new ways to keep our most intimate relationships alive in the face of death. With Final Words and Legacy Letters, Mary encourages us to face the inevitability of death and loss together by writing to each other our love, appreciation, amends, and forgiveness before it's too late.

Shortly after I was diagnosed with cancer and was lost in my sickness, my son read me a letter he had written to me. His words reached across the chasm separating us. His words reached my heart. Read Mary's book. Write your letters. I'm working on mine."

—David Treadway, Ph.D., family therapist and author of *Intimacy, Change, and other Therapeutic Mysteries* and *Dead Reckoning: A Therapist Confronts his own Grief*

"We live each moment just a heartbeat away from death, at risk of losing everyone we love, or once loved. We can't change this sobering fact of life, but we can ensure that on any given day we have said the things that we would most want the important people in our lives to know. *In Nothing Left Unsaid*, Mary Polce-Lynch conveys timeless wisdom and offers practical tools for affirming relationships and strengthening bonds of friendship and love. This book is a treasure for anyone who is mortal, or loves someone who is . . ."

—Ira Byock, M.D. Director of Palliative Medicine and Professor, Dartmouth Medical School, author of *Dying Well* and *The Four Things That Matter Most*

About the Author

Mary Polce-Lynch, PhD, works at Randolph-Macon College as assistant director of the Counseling Center and visiting assistant professor of psychology. She is a developmental psychologist and licensed professional counselor also certified as a school psychologist and teacher. Her professional interests focus on lifespan development in the areas of psychotherapy, gender, and emotional expression, and her activities include conducting workshops and research. Dr. Polce-Lynch has published for professional and general audiences throughout her career and has been recognized for academic and professional achievements. She is a member of the American Association of Pastoral Counselors and the American Psychological Association.

NOTHING LEFT UNSAID

ALSO BY MARY POLCE-LYNCH

Boy Talk: How You Can Help Your Son Express His Emotions

NOTHING LEFT UNSAID

Creating a Healing Legacy

ᔑᐸ *with* ᔑᐸ

Final Words and Letters

MARY POLCE-LYNCH, PhD

MARLOWE & COMPANY

NEW YORK

NOTHING LEFT UNSAID:
Creating a Healing Legacy with Final Words and Letters

Copyright © 2006 by Mary Polce-Lynch

Published by
Marlowe & Company
An Imprint of Avalon Publishing Group Incorporated
245 West 17th Street, 11th floor
New York, NY 10011-5300

AVALON
publishing group incorporated

Grateful acknowledgment to the following for permission to use previously published material:

Adam and Joey Riklis's story, from *Small Miracles,* Copyright © 1997 by Yitta Halberstam Mandelbaum and Judith Frankel Leventhal. Used by permission of Adams Media. All rights reserved.

Final letter of PFC Jesse Givens, permission granted by his widow, Melissa Givens.

Henry Potter's Will, permission granted by transcriber, Laura Powers.

"The Ethical Will" by Mike Moldevan, permission granted by Caregiver Network, Inc.

Library of Congress Cataloging-in-Publication Data
Polce-Lynch, Mary.
    Nothing Left Unsaid: creating a healing legacy with final words and letters / Mary Polce-Lynch.
    p.cm.
    Includes bibliographical references.
    ISBN 1-56924-321-2
    1. Bereavement. 2. Closure (Rhetoric) 3. Wills, Ethical—Authorship.
    I. Title.
    BF575.G7.P625 2006
    155.9'37—dc22

                                                              2005031181

ISBN-13: 978-1-56924-321-3

9 8 7 6 5 4 3 2 1

Designed by Maria E. Torres
Printed in the United States of America

For my family

In memory of Anthony H. Polce Sr.

Contents

CHAPTER 1
WHY CREATE A HEALING LEGACY?

Ten Days . . . Much Left Unsaid . . . Deconstructing Final Good-byes . . . Contemporary Final Messages . . . The Last Will and Testament: Then and Now . . . Paying It Forward

CHAPTER 2
MOVING BEYOND RESISTANCE TO BENEFITS

Benefits for the Writer . . . Overcoming Inner Resistance: You and Your Shadow . . . Grief Connections . . . The Role of Temperament and Personality . . . Making a Real Difference

CHAPTER 3
FINAL GOOD-BYES ACROSS CULTURES

Death Denial . . . Early Death Education Lessons . . . Why Think about Death Preparation Differently? . . . Death Preparation Practices in the United States . . . Cross-Cultural Death Perspectives . . . A New Cross-Cultural Social Norm

CHAPTER 8
❧ PARENT LEGACIES ❧
pg 173

Developmental Perspectives . . . Developmental Overview . . . Transcending Fear and Death Denial: Final Words to Children . . . Important Writing Decisions . . . One Parent's Final Words . . . Writing Legacy Letters to Young Children . . . Writing Final Words and Legacy Letters to Adult Children . . . Explaining Final Words . . . For Grandparents . . . Summary for Parents

CHAPTER 9
❧ A DIFFERENT KIND OF INHERITANCE ❧
pg 197

Questions and Answers about Writing Final Words and Legacy Letters . . . Other Types of Healing Legacies . . . Forgiveness in Healing Legacies . . . Final Thoughts on Final Messages

Author's Note

To protect privacy and any breach of confidence, stories and letters about individual people in this book are either composites or hypothetical accounts. The themes and experiences conveyed, however, are accurate. The exception to this confidentiality includes quotations attributed to specific authors and stories or accounts in which individuals requested that their identities be made known.

Introduction

IMAGINE SOMEONE IN your life suddenly dies. It could be a parent, spouse, partner, child, or friend. Their unexpected death left no time to say good-bye . . . no time to express love, forgiveness, or unspoken hopes and dreams. You wanted and needed these words.

Now envision a different ending. It could be days after the death of your loved one, weeks after the distracting details, or perhaps even a year later. You are ready now. Sitting in a quiet and safe place, you open a letter written to you from the person who died. Long before the death, that person set aside thoughtful time to reflect on his or her life and relationships. The letter contains heartfelt expressions and final messages. These words amaze you. Though your soul is weighed down by this final good-bye, you begin to feel lifted. The comfort you experience holding this paper between your fingers, reading it over and over and over, is almost beyond description. *It's just what you needed.*

Despite the fact that each of us will die sometime, or that hundreds of thousands of people die suddenly every year in the United States alone, most cultures do not have an established ritual to ensure personal messages of good-bye. After an adult dies, the final written communication is usually the formal last will and testament. And no established ritual exists for children's good-byes. It does not have to be this way. Death—sudden or expected—is real. And a final personal message can be just as real. But for this idea to become a healing ritual, each of us must look beyond *who gets what* in legal wills to *what's left unsaid* in relationships.

People may initially resist the idea of writing a final message while they are very much alive. This is to be expected. No one likes to think about death. But when we consider the fuller context of writing final good-byes, the message extends far beyond death. It's not about dying; it is about healing grief and bringing deeper meaning to life in the present.

If you think about it, final personal messages can be written to loved ones at any time. We don't have to wait until the end of life or the onset of a terminal illness. And anyone can write them, even children and teens. On the simplest level, all it takes is recognizing the significance of this ritual and then participating in it. But on a broader cultural level, a shift is required. I visualize this shift as a "handshake" between acknowledging mortality and empathizing with grief. Indeed, if we accept our inevitable death and empathize with the pain of those we will leave behind, we make the necessary connection that creates a healing legacy.

There is no way to erase grief. But there are ways to facilitate the healing and adjustment process. As our attention shifts from bequeathing possessions to creating healing legacies, a guide is needed. And *Final Words,* a narrative written for loved ones to be read after we die, is one way. The heart of this writing is to honor our relationships. Final Words can convey expressions of love, affirmation, regret, life lessons, hopes, wishes, forgiveness, personal legacy, blessing, and good-bye. I encourage people to write these messages when they are well rather than at the end of their life. In addition, you may wish to write a *Legacy Letter,* which conveys similar sentiments, to a loved one before his or her death. Unlike Final Words, the Legacy Letter is intended to be read while both the writer and reader are still alive. Taken together, Final Words and Legacy Letters ensure that nothing is left unsaid.

It may be clear how writing Final Words can facilitate the healing process and provide tangible closure for the bereaved, but writing these messages can also benefit the writer in many ways. As we reckon with death and ponder what we've given and received in relationships, we may unexpectedly glean what's missing. This reflection process can deepen and enrich relationships *now*. We also contemplate the type of legacy we want to pass on to children, grandchildren, friends, and the larger community. But the benefits of reflection don't end there. Writing Final Words can help clarify purpose and deepen life's meaning in the broadest sense as well as in daily life. Everyone may not experience these same benefits. Some people may become aware of other benefits, while others may initially have difficulty with the writing process. Similar to the way we cannot apply group research results to individual people, information conveyed in books may not apply directly to everyone in the same way.

Every culture has a procedural way to settle estates and material possessions. Cultures also have specific funerary rites. But rituals that ensure a final good-bye do not exist in a formal way, and the reasons for this vary. It may be the "death denial" that resides deep in our psyches; no one wants to think about their own death or the inevitable passing of their loved ones. The absence of ritual may also be due to tradition, religious belief, and tribal custom. Or perhaps it is a combination of all these reasons. While some practices convey personal legacy after death, they have not been broad or inclusive. Indeed, the majority of us don't receive written personal messages from loved ones after they have died. Most people do not know what to say or how to have a face-to-face final farewell. And even when we do say good-bye, a lingering need for a tangible symbol can emerge as time goes on. Months after my friend's parent died from a terminal illness, several siblings found themselves needing "more." Though verbal good-byes were said, they described how a personal letter—something they could hold in their hand—would have helped their grief.

Since we all know that we will die eventually, each of us has the opportunity to plan ahead and craft final messages to loved ones in the event of sudden death, terminal illness, or the end of a long and well-lived life. In the absence of a final personal message, it can be disorienting when the last communication between you and your loved ones is a formal will, communicated in legal terminology. People yearn for something to help transcend their grief. Final Words do this and more.

Writing Legacy Letters to loved ones who may die first can also help with aspects of grief related to closure. By affirming the life of elderly parents or grandparents, terminally ill loved ones, or those going into harm's way, we may reassure them of core questions that people reflect on at this time: *Was I a good son or daughter? Was I a good spouse or partner? Was I a good parent? Did I make the world a better place? Did I do enough? Am I forgiven?* Legacy Letters can also express gratitude, forgiveness, and treasured memories. Think about how comforting it would be for a loved one to receive a letter that acknowledged all of this. Think too about how peaceful you would feel knowing that you expressed everything you wanted them to know. Let the impact of this healing legacy sink in for a moment. Then consider how comforting it would be to *receive* a letter like this yourself.

Legacy Letters can be given any time to express intimate or important thoughts. It doesn't have to be at the end of life. Parents may write letters to their children to celebrate milestones, birthdays, or graduations. Or adult children may write letters to their parents after recovering from adolescent rebellion, when starting or finishing college, or after becoming a parent themselves. Missives like these have been written throughout history and stand on their own as a blessing. I refer to them as Legacy Letters because they help us define and transcend ourselves, the way true legacies do. And in the absence of exchanging last good-byes with a loved one, they may also eventually come to serve as Final Words.

Nothing Left Unsaid outlines a need for the ritual of writing final personal messages and then guides readers through the process. Although contemporary greeting cards express every possible sentiment, there is absolutely nothing that can replace a personal and unique letter to a loved one or from a loved one to you. Our words have great power. The simplest and most direct statements can make a life worth living. These basic messages contribute to our wholeness as human and spiritual beings. Yet the simplest things often go unspoken in daily life: words of appreciation, acceptance, apology, forgiveness. These are powerful words that people need to say and hear.

The structure of this book includes the big picture as well as the details. Beginning chapters provide a rationale for writing Final Words and Legacy Letters. Information about cultural and emotional aspects of death and grief is included. Middle chapters provide "how to" steps that address details about writing Final Words and Legacy Letters. Subsequent chapters are written for specific reader populations (women, men, and parents). The final chapter focuses on specific "what ifs" *(What if I don't know what to say? What if I feel too angry or resentful?)* and then zooms out to integrate the meaning and expected outcomes of writing final messages.

Writing Final Words and Legacy Letters is a form of emotional expression that extends into death preparation. While I have been interested in emotional expression throughout my career as a psychotherapist and developmental psychologist, I didn't think about writing final personal messages until after my father's sudden death. He was unable to say good-bye and express final wishes to his family and loved ones, and we were unable to affirm his life and express final words to him. But a healing legacy serendipitously began when I discovered two old letters that he and I had exchanged earlier in our lives— and that I had since forgotten. The letters were simple, direct, and powerful. And they were concrete proof of what had *not* been left unsaid. Surely I could have begun healing sooner if I had known these letters existed when my father died. So not long after his death, I sat down and wrote personal letters to my family as a type of healing legacy in case of my own sudden death. I began sharing the idea of final messages with people and their positive responses eventually led to this book. As more people decide to write, I welcome suggestions, questions, and any other feedback about the idea of writing final messages as a healing legacy.

Since death is real, creating a healing legacy can be just as real. Perhaps the first generation who receives Final Words and Legacy Letters will continue the tradition. And perhaps the benefits that writers experience will also help maintain the ritual. Indeed, the insights gathered from writing final messages can be the kindling to start heartfelt changes in behavior and relationships—now. So while at first glance it may seem like writing final messages is about facing death, it may be more about facing life.

Terrorist threats, car accidents, natural disasters, and age-old types of sudden death surround all of us today. Ritualizing final messages could transform how we die—and live.

I invite you to participate in the writing process and hope *Nothing Left Unsaid* helps you find the words to create a healing legacy for your loved ones.

Don't let fear and death denial get in the way. If you don't write your Final Words and Legacy Letters, who will?

CHAPTER 1

WHY CREATE A HEALING LEGACY?

SHARING CERTAIN MOMENTS in life can transform people. But it's easy to miss those moments. The reason we miss the moments never ends up mattering, though. What matters is just not missing them.

I know this firsthand. My father gave up cigarettes in his early sixties at the first sign of heart trouble. His decision bought us all two more decades to spend together. This may seem generous enough, but it wasn't. A sudden and fatal heart attack eventually took his life and prevented final good-byes with his family and friends. We missed the moments. But this story is much more than a grieving daughter's regrets. It is ultimately about the healing power of writing final messages.

My father was a good man. Known to his family and friends as Tony, he was intelligent and, in his younger days, was a city golf champion. He was also the kindest person I have ever known. The relationship between my father and me could be described as simpatico. While we didn't agree on everything, I always knew he was in my corner. Over the years he taught my siblings and me about the importance of many things—working hard, being responsible, and taking care of family. He also told great bedtime stories and made really good spaghetti sauce. My father was passing on lasting family values, but what I treasured most was simply his love.

The only one of three children to permanently move away from home, I could feel his love following me each time I drifted a little farther south, until I eventually planted roots in central Virginia to raise my own family. The relationship between my father and me remained close despite the geographical separation. I thought I was living in such a way that if any particular day was suddenly his last, there would be no regrets. Yeah, right. I had allowed a new job and the multitasking madness of today's culture absorb my attention during what would be his final year of life. This painful fact compounded my initial grief. It wasn't until months later that I discovered the letters he and I had exchanged—the ones that would eventually serve as healing legacies.

Ten Days

My father had a severe heart attack in November 2002. He was transported via a Mercy Flight helicopter from the local hospital in Geneva, New York, to a cardiac intensive care unit in Rochester, seventy miles away. There we would soon learn that four of his main arteries were almost totally blocked. We would also learn that he had suffered at least one previous heart attack, probably around the same time that he and my mother, Esther, learned that her cancer had returned with a vengeance.

My husband, John, and I were at our daughters' swim meet the night of my father's November heart attack. While these meets are always lengthy and tiring (for parents), I was more tired than usual and couldn't catch my breath. I found out why after returning home. There was a message on the answering machine from my brother-in-law: "Tony had a serious heart attack . . . he's alive but in serious condition." Trying to fall asleep that night, a strange and cold heaviness began filling my gut.

I hugged my husband good-bye at the Richmond airport before dawn and was holding my dad's hand in Rochester by noon. For the next few hours, I rubbed his clammy forehead and kept reassuring him that Esther was okay and that we all loved him. I also prayed out loud. Despite being heavily sedated and having an intubation tube in his throat, he mouthed the prayers with me *word for word*. He also kept asking when he could go home. That's Tony—he loved his family and home fiercely. I knew he wouldn't die there.

With hour-by-hour recovery, my father eventually became strong enough to be transferred to a cardiac rehabilitation center back home. By now, my family and I had learned that Tony's arteries could not be repaired with stents. The damage was too old and severe. Instead he would continue to be treated with diet and pills and rely on the skinny and less-efficient helper arteries that had developed over time. This condition sounded fatal to me, but no one ever described it as such—not one doctor, nurse, or rehabilitation therapist. And certainly not Tony. His sole focus was getting better so he could take care of my mother. And so that became the whole family's focus, too. My sister, Peggy, bought him his first pair of sweatpants for rehab and he got a kick out of wearing them. Back at the house, my brother, Tony, made and installed stair railings to the second floor, where the bedrooms are (my dad kept marveling at those beautiful oak railings). By the end of his hospital rehabilitation, Tony had successfully relearned balancing, walking, and stair climbing.

While continuing to recover at home, Tony also learned how to keep daily track of more than two dozen pills. Esther helped as much as she could, but because of her heavy chemotherapy, she was extremely fatigued. She was also frightened. What worried her most was the foreboding sense that *she* might die first. If something happened to her, she knew my father couldn't take care of himself yet.

Making daily phone calls and paying hospital bills were all I could do from far away—that and praying. So when I visited my parents over the winter holidays, I ran every errand I could, hunted down every no-salt/low-fat species of food, and searched for new pants to fit Tony's shrinking body. I left exhausted but satisfied that I had helped in some way. But I never just sat quietly with my dad. Since I was planning to return for my parents' fiftieth wedding anniversary in a month, I let go of that regret. But that heavy sensation inside me wouldn't go away. Like a blinking red light on an answering machine, it seemed to be telling me something. But I never got the message.

I called my father every day after that visit. *I love you* from both of us ended each conversation. He was saying this to everyone lately. As if it might mend a heart about to stop—or break. I picked up the phone on January 13 to make my daily call and to say that I had just found some great walking shoes for him. Ones that could replace the ancient clodhoppers he'd been wearing for far too long. I didn't finish making that phone call. Instead, I put the receiver down and mailed the shoe catalog with a yellow Post-it note stuck to page nine, *Buy this pair, Dad!* After all, Tony could live well past ninety like his mother did. How could I know the future? So I decided to let my parents get back to normal and stop the daily check-ins.

That same January day, my father finally got permission from his doctor to drive again. Tony had made it all the way back. His focus and tenacity weren't limited to winning golf tournaments. He never gave up at life, either. My mother tells me how proud he was for regaining full independence for them. She says that on their last afternoon together, as they planned the next day's grocery trip, they were like giddy newlyweds.

Tony rose early the next day. He ate breakfast, swallowed his plethora of pills, and stepped onto the porch to sweep away the light snow that had fallen overnight. Always doing small but kind things for others, he did this so the paperboy wouldn't slip. My dad never came back in. Around 7:30 AM, a neighbor found him lying across the front porch. Tony had been the greeter and guardian of this home for forty-three years. There wasn't a more appropriate place for him to die.

I had always wished that my dad would have his family circled around him as he passed from this life to the next. So when I first learned he died alone, I felt as though we had failed him. Yet when my mother gazed at his face as his body lay still on the front porch, she described it as being more peaceful than she had ever seen it. This single image tethered me to the earth during the long drive north for his funeral— that and believing that somehow his parents and brothers who had died decades ago *did* circle around when he passed.

Around the same time that morning, I was sitting in a rocking chair across from my daughter. While we were chatting about school, I felt my heart jolt. This brief sensation was immediately followed by a peaceful warmth. Not one to notice small things so early in the morning, my daughter asked why I had just put my hand over my heart. At the time I didn't think much of it and said I didn't know. When my mother called at 8:10 AM and wailed, "Daddy's gone," that strange heaviness I had been carrying inside immediately exploded and began filling every cell of my body.

My parents' fiftieth wedding anniversary came ten days after he died. Had I been able to see my father again, I would have been able to say, *I love you, Dad. You're the best father I could have ever had. I was always proud to be your daughter. Thank you for how you took care of our family.* My father needed to hear these words as much as I needed to say them. But his death came too unexpectedly for us to share that moment.

Family and friends gathered at my sister's home after the funeral. My father had saved a 1971 bottle of Canadian Club whiskey he had won in the Snowshoe Golf Tournament. He always warned us not to touch it until after he died. Somehow in the midst of our trauma and grief, my brother remembered the whiskey. So I wrote a toast to honor—and say good-bye to—my father. As my brother got everyone's attention, I looked out the kitchen window. A baptismal white snow had just started falling. It seemed to warm the frigid air. We raised our glasses like a flock of birds taking flight . . . "To Tony!" The gentle spirit of the whiskey and the memory of this kind man warmed us all inside.

Much Left Unsaid

Although I am a private person, I shared this personal story because if the custom of writing Final Words had been established, I believe my dad would have written to his family. Just as important, because of his advancing age and declining health, we would have written Legacy Letters of affirmation to him. But due to sudden death, final words were never exchanged between my father and his wife of fifty years or with any of his family and lifelong friends. We all still ache about this. Though we have a lifetime of memories and his kind legacy to (try to) emulate, we would have given anything to know that nothing had been left unsaid.

Most cultures establish legal rituals for distributing personal belongings after death. This usually takes the form of a document like the last will and testament. While such documents bring closure to material inheritance, they do not address emotional inheritance, especially if a sudden death occurs and there is no chance to say good-bye.

A Grief Journey

During the first year after my father's death, an unexpected discovery helped begin healing my grief. I found several forgotten letters that he and I had exchanged decades ago. These correspondences essentially served as his Final Words to me and as my Legacy Letter to him. While neither completely erased my grief, both provided a comfort I could not have imagined. It is from this grace-filled experience that the idea of writing final messages occurred to me.

I experienced more pain—and healing—as I continued along my grief journey. As a counselor I knew that sudden death was traumatic. But I didn't really *know it as a person.* Before my father died, I assumed that our close relationship over the years meant that we had said everything we needed to say. This certainty faded like shadows into evening. Even though I am a rational middle-aged adult, two days after his funeral I found myself panicking. I could only focus on the past year, when I had been so busy. I worried that he didn't know how much he was loved and that I thought he was a great dad. I worried that much had been left unsaid.

So on that same day, I frantically began searching for something to tell me otherwise. I didn't know what I was looking for, but if it existed, I knew it would be in the bedroom. I started in his dresser, then his closet. Eventually, I moved to a dark pine nightstand beside his bed. It had a small drawer on top with a cabinet door below. Before that moment I had never thought much about that nightstand; now it had become a hope chest. Opening the drawer, I noticed a couple of recent greeting cards. I closed it in disappointment. But as I unlatched the cabinet door, I saw a leaning pile of more than a hundred greeting cards. It appeared as if my father had saved every card that anyone ever gave him! Buried in this surprising cache was a card that immediately began easing my fear. It was a Father's Day card I remembered carefully picking out for him two years ago. He was in his mid-eighties, and I knew that with each advancing year there would be fewer opportunities to pick out a Father's Day card for him. The one I chose had expressed my love, respect, and gratitude in phrases that seemed to capture the essence of his kind character. I had never felt so relieved about finding a greeting card.

With this tangible reassurance that my father knew he was loved and appreciated, my anxiety settled down. But strong negative feelings sporadically returned. Grief often comes in bursts like that. Only this time I was more sad than worried as I found myself longing for words *from him to me.* So two months later, back home in Virginia, I climbed my attic steps in search again. I didn't know what for, but somehow I knew where to look. When I opened the attic door, I went directly to a black footlocker from college.

Among cardboard boxes and that dry, sweet attic smell, I kneeled down in front of the footlocker. I unfastened the tarnished latches and lifted the heavy lid. Hidden beneath a pile of journals and photo albums, I found the small cedar box where I kept cherished mementos. I passed over each one: a discolored photo of the Shenandoah Valley, a card from an inspirational youth minister, notes from the first students I taught. Then I found a white folded letter. I held my breath as I opened it. It was a letter that my father had written to me almost twenty years ago. In it, he thanked me for a recent visit. He acknowledged that although I was a self-sufficient person, he and my mom would always be there for me. Toward the end of the letter, he had written about our family. He expressed pride and love for each one by name. I now found myself crying hard as I held his words between my fingers. And yet somehow, I also felt so happy. It was as if he had written this letter, and I had saved it, for this very purpose.

But my grief didn't end there. And neither did the healing. A year later while visiting my mother, I returned to that same pine nightstand in his bedroom. (Yes, I was still searching.) I pulled out several greeting cards midway through the leaning stack. This batch included a card from one of his brothers, my sister, and me. They were not inspirational or comforting, so I slipped them back into their chronological place and pulled out a few more. I found another Father's Day card that I had given him, circa 1980 in design. It was double-paged and the insert had a daughter-to-father message that expressed pride in having a father like him. Each special message I found in these cards helped me realize what I would have said to him in a final good-bye. So I took that card home with me as I had done with some of those I had found on my first visit.

With this growing satellite collection of greeting cards back in Virginia, I decided to put them to good use as bookmarks (a little large, but surprisingly functional.) While I was reading one night, something made me look at the newly retrieved card/bookmark. To my surprise, as I was holding the card in my hands, a letter slid out and fell onto my lap. I didn't recognize the letter but the handwriting was mine. Then I had a flashback to the summer I graduated from college. I remembered writing a letter of thanksgiving to my father for all he had done for me in college—and in life—as

I was about to launch from home to career. The letter expressed every word I would have wanted him to know at the end of his life. Elated and grateful for yet another amazing "find," I also noticed, once again, how my grief was lessened by the pure exchange of words.

Death has an ephemeral quality, much like life. So it's not surprising that we long for something tangible from loved ones after they are gone. But this need to have and hold *words*—both to and from my father—still wasn't entirely clear to me until another family death. My mother-in-law, Clare Norris, died just several months after my father. She was a remarkable woman who raised ten children and survived lymphoma. But after a lengthy remission it returned when she was in her seventies. Clare's courageous attempts to find a cure through invasive treatments were not successful; the cancer sadly and slowly became terminal. Because of the nature and pace of her illness, Clare's family had almost two months to affirm her life and to exchange good-byes. Though this is certainly not a long time, it is a generous amount when compared to no time. And while it is always traumatic at some level when a loved one dies, the ending to my mother-in-law's life was marked more by peacefulness than by the shock of a sudden death. Family members were able to express final words of affirmation and good-bye to Clare. And she didn't spend her last moments alone.

The endings to my father's and my mother-in-law's lives were so different. I now realize that my unrelenting search for some type of closure explained why I wouldn't throw away the "to do" list that I found on my father's dresser while we were "taking care of his things." Seemingly meaningless notes: *Check furnace filter; Fix porch step; Anniversary card.* Certainly not words of good-bye. So why did I keep them? To me, they were his ideas and I could hold them between my fingers. Moreover, because the words existed, it meant he had been here. Staring at these slips of paper one day made me wonder, *What would it be like to hold personal words of good-bye from my father? What would it have been like to know with certainty, when my father died, that we had left nothing unsaid?*

I will never know the answer to these questions. But I hope the story of my father's death provides a real answer to this chapter's rhetorical title, "Why Create a Healing Legacy?"

Deconstructing Final Good-byes

Participating in final good-byes with our loved ones appears to be of universal importance, yet it has not become a universal custom. When searching for information about what people say—or need to say—to one another in final good-byes, I did not find anything that applied to the general population. Instead, information was located in three specific populations: hospice patient's memorial legacies, Jewish ethical wills, and wartime letters from men and women in the armed forces.

I was initially frustrated by the lack of existing information for the general population. My training as a social scientist taught me to begin studying a subject by researching the existing literature. But if no such literature existed, how would I proceed? Then I became excited. If the custom of writing final good-byes didn't exist yet for the general population, then perhaps it was time to encourage the practice.

According to Helen Fitzgerald, a grief expert, the importance of saying good-bye lies in the closure of one relationship to welcome the next.[1] In the hospice field, preparing a final good-bye is referred to by many names: creating an oral history, memorial, personal legacy, or final message. A recent hospice study examined the effects of a specific type of final good-bye in "dignity therapy," an intervention designed to address existential and psychosocial distress of hospice patients.[2] Part of this therapy involves inviting patients to discuss issues that matter most to them or that they would most want remembered. These conversations are transcribed, edited, and returned to the patient to leave to their loved ones. Results of this study indicated that these patients report a significant reduction in a sense of suffering paired with a significant increase in a sense of meaning and purpose. These findings lend empirical support for the benefits of final good-byes.

After reviewing information from the hospice literature and ethical wills, I discovered that final good-byes often include the following elements: reviewing life accomplishments, recognizing the importance of family and friends, affirming the unique qualities of the person and the relationship, recalling specific memories, conveying values, passing on family history or legacy, expressing love, naming regrets, asking for or granting forgiveness, and describing the future.[3, 4, 5] This future element might include acknowledging how life will be different and how the deceased would like to be remembered, as well as conveying specific hopes or wishes for those who are left behind. My research also revealed that final good-byes can be expressed in many different forms, such as oral, written, videotape, or digital. They may even take the form of a photo album.

In the following excerpt, Helen Fitzgerald describes an oral final good-bye with her father. It represents several elements identified in this section:

> One of the best gifts for dying patients is reassuring them that they will be fondly remembered. When my father was dying, I realized that I had not said "good-bye" to him yet, so I went to visit him. During that visit we talked about our life together: our horseback riding days and square dancing on our horses. I recounted the important things he taught me, which I passed on to my children, who are now teaching their children. When I left him, I had a lasting feeling of peace.[6]

Oral good-byes can indeed be extremely satisfying and peaceful. Yet there is something about being able to hold a personal letter or note, written by a loved one from whom we are separated, that is both comforting and permanent in a way that the spoken word is not.

It is vital to emphasize that the final good-bye is not a one-way communication. The dying need to know certain things from us just as we have a need to express certain things to them. Most humans do not want to say good-bye to people they love for lengthy periods, much less for eternity. The inconceivable nature of death—and beyond—makes it difficult to wrap our minds around a final good-bye. Yet it would seem important for those left behind to not only have closure, but to have a personal connection that transcends legal documents and wills. Final Words and Legacy Letters serve this purpose. Without a written narrative from the one who died, loved ones are often left with unanswered questions. Indeed, certain questions can only be answered by certain people.

Contemporary Final Messages

Death preparation in mainstream United States culture is formal and businesslike. We take stock of our material possessions, we meet with an attorney, we write a legal will that describes who gets what, and then we're done. These actions allow us to think we have taken care of death preparation. We believe this, in part, because our culture has no further expectations in this regard. There are many potentially negative outcomes related to this manner of dealing with death. One is that by focusing on the legal aspect of death and the bequeathing of material possessions, we don't take care of the *relational* aspects of death—how our death will emotionally affect loved ones. Another negative outcome is the myopic focus on the legal aspects of death preparation. We file death away with the last will and testament and push it out of our minds as if it didn't exist. When it comes, we keep hoping and praying (as I did for my father) that our loved one will live—right up until their last breath.

This section began by exposing how we primarily limit ourselves to material inheritance and ignore personal legacies. As all of this is brought to light, it may seem obvious that personal and final good-byes are important—perhaps even necessary. But mainstream culture has not yet developed a custom or ritual that supports and ensures this. There are many forms of resistance to this concept that are exposed in this book. In order to begin considering the idea of a new cultural ritual, it makes sense here to become more familiar with current customs involving death preparation and emotional closure: hospice care, ethical wills, and wartime letters.

A Closer Look at Hospice Good-byes

Most people are aware that hospice and palliative care are now available to terminally ill patients and their families in many countries, and that hospice is one of the leaders in guiding the final good-byes between terminally ill patients and their loved ones. Though recent books about creating rituals at the end of life are also reaching the mainstream population, most of us initially resist facing death, whether we are alive and well or alive and dying.

Dr. Beth Gill is a sociology professor at Randolph-Macon College and an expert on death memorialization strategies in the United States whose work sheds light on some of our interpersonal resistance to final good-byes. Gill has found that it is difficult to encourage dying individuals to memorialize themselves through a written narrative.[7] She states that hospice volunteers are often instructed to encourage the dying and their families to create a memorial, either written or oral, before a person dies. Yet Gill's research indicates that this task can become challenging because families are often fraught with conflict and tension based on past occurrences, the very things that would be remembered if such an oral or written endeavor were undertaken. In addition to this resistance, Gill also notes that the very act of creating memorials and developing oral histories during a stressful time (such as terminal illness) is incredibly difficult. As the disease progresses, less energy is available for such a task, making it counterproductive at times.

Just as terminally ill patients need to say good-bye to loved ones, it is important for loved ones to honor the lives of the terminally ill and say good-bye to them. Yet this does not always happen. Perhaps as loved ones keep hope alive, they can also affirm and celebrate the lives of the terminally ill. Such words can be spoken and written. I advocate for writing a Legacy Letter (discussed in chapter 5), as it allows for more reflection. In some ways, writing a letter to a loved one who will die is like "moving up" the funeral homily to the present. This way, loved ones can be affirmed and nothing is left unsaid.

Interest in Ethical Wills

Though mainstream U.S. culture does not yet have a ritual for preparing final good-byes, it may be evolving as evidenced in the growing interest in ethical wills. I first learned about ethical wills in a feature article by Karen Cheney in the AARP's (American Association of Retired Persons) magazine.[8] The ethical will grew out of a tradition within the Jewish culture and has served as a final personal message written to loved ones by an elderly person. It is typically a memoir to a whole family. A close friend, an attorney, or a trusted family member is told about the ethical will, its location, and to whom it should be delivered. Ethical wills can be traced to biblical times, beginning as an oral tradition and then changing to written form. Cheney cites the book of Genesis for what may be the first ethical will, as Jacob summons his twelve sons to his deathbed to tell stories about each son, discuss their futures, and pass on some of his wisdom.

Ethical wills are traditionally written at the end of life and read after the writer's death. Recent practices include writing at turning points of a person's life and sharing the words with loved ones while the writer is still alive. Barry Baines, author of a popular book on ethical wills,[9] decided to present his own ethical will to his children when they were teenagers: "When I finished writing it, I felt an incredible peace of mind, a sense of accomplishment . . . I also realized that I'd gone public with what I think is important. It forces me to think twice and walk the talk."[10] Rabbi Jack Reimer describes ethical wills as being both difficult to write and difficult to read. But he also states there is much good that can come from this challenge. He suggests that as writers reflect inward and evaluate personal values and beliefs, the process of honest self-examination naturally includes seeing and admitting failures along with successes.[11] It also helps a person consider what really counts over the course of one's life.

Recently published books and various Web sites on ethical wills reflect increased interest in leaving personal legacies.[12, 13] To illustrate the spirit of ethical wills, here is an example from "The Ethical Will," an article by Mike Moldevan posted on the Caregiver Network, Inc., Web site.[14] It is a fictional ethical will, and the hypothetical writer is a father and grandfather:

My dear family,

In writing this, I have no premonitions of an early demise or of other untoward events. On the other hand, and as you note from when this was written, I am now well along in years. It is time, perhaps, for me to contemplate once again what I've done and left undone as a father and as a grandfather. I say "once again" but this time my advanced age presses me to record my thoughts for all of you to read or listen to at a suitable time after I am gone. . . .

I hope my disposition of substance did not create ill feelings; the decisions seemed reasonable when I made them. Should you feel like trading back and forth later on, feel free; you've all been doing that with gifts from Mom—or Grandma—and me since you were knee-high. What I've stipulated as going to you grand-kids should not be sold or switched about until you've reached 18. I think you'll better understand why you got what you did when you're older. You might even conclude Grandpa was right—again.

I am far more concerned that you hear me on a matter far more important than mere substance. As a salaried worker, and later as a businessman, my outlook on the world was pragmatic and, I hope, not overly sanctimonious. I recall being referred to more than once as a practical guy. And yet, in these latter years, I've questioned both my doubts and my certainties with a deeper awareness than I feel I've had previously; perhaps it's an expanded intuition and sensitivity that accompanies aging.

I've come to accept that there is purpose to our universe, and therefore purpose to us who are of its essence. To me, to be with-out purpose is to be without meaning; all of life, all of us, would be meaningless. I reject a meaningless life—a meaningless family. I hope that, in time, each of you will also accept that our lives have meaning, therefore purpose, and guide yourselves and your progeny accordingly.

Live together in harmony. Consider the family when an issue foments stresses among you. Help each other in times of need and turmoil even though you reside at great distances and your lifestyles and outlooks on life differ greatly.

Honor and care for Mom—Grandma. Make her old age happy years, as far as it is in your power to do so. She more than deserves such consideration from each of you. You have heard Mom gently reproach me at times about my not giving enough attention to my children and grandchildren. She always wanted more for each of you. Be worthy of her devotion.

Carry the family heritage with dignity. Though you discard customs and rituals you consider trivial, bear in mind many have come down the centuries and withstood the tests of time and travail.

Do not mourn me. I have enjoyed my life. Move on, using for good purposes the knowledge and skills you have acquired over the years. You will serve your family best by serving humankind.

Remember me affectionately as your Dad and Grandpa

An ethical will like this is meaningful on many levels. The writer's words convey a combination of wisdom, regret, and contentment. There are also specific requests and future wishes. How reassuring and comforting it would be for a family to read this and know with certainty that their "Dad and Grandpa" was happy with his life—perhaps it would be healing, too.

The reason for the increased interest in ethical wills may be related to the presence of terrorism in our lives, as well as an increase in death and dying education over the past few decades. In addition, those affected by the sudden deaths of loved ones often become motivated to ensure their progeny have a final good-bye.

Wartime Letters to Loved Ones

Men and women who go into harm's way for their country are catapulted into thinking about their mortality and how it will affect loved ones. Some choose to go forward without looking back, while others provide a final good-bye—just in case. Such intimate letters and correspondences provide us all not only with the necessary reminder of our own mortality, but also with a greater understanding of the need for—and the substance of—final good-byes.

Michelle Norris interviewed Bill Couturie, producer and director of the television documentary *Last Letters Home: Voices of American Troops from the Battlefields of Iraq*.[15] This documentary tells stories of the families of eight men and two women who were killed in the Iraq war. Spouses and parents describe intimate final e-mails and letters received after news of their loved one's death. Private First Class Jesse A. Givens, stationed in Iraq, is one of the soldiers featured in the documentary. He was killed May 1, 2003, soon after arriving in Iraq. He left behind his pregnant wife, Melissa Givens, and his son Dakota, who was six years old at the time. According to several accounts, PFC Givens wrote several letters to his family. His final letter arrived home about a month after his funeral and shortly after his wife gave birth to their son Carson.

22 April '03

My family:

I never thought that I would be writing a letter like this. I really don't know where to start. I've been getting bad feelings, though and, well, if you are reading this. . . .

I am forever in debt to you, Dakota, and the Bean. I searched all my life for a dream and I found it in you. I would like to think that I made a positive difference in your lives. I will never be able to make up for the bad. I am so sorry. The happiest moments in my life all deal with my little family. I will always have with me the small moments we all shared. The moments when you quit taking life so serious and smiled. The sounds of a beautiful boy's laughter or the simple nudge of a baby unborn. You will never know how complete you have made me. Each one of you. You saved me from loneliness and taught me how to think beyond myself. You taught me how to live and to love. You opened my eyes to a world I never dreamed existed. I am proud of you. Stay on the path you chose. Never lose sight of what is important again, you and our babies. . . .

I will always be there with you, Melissa. I will always want you, need you, and love you in my heart, mind and soul. Do me a favor, after you tuck Toad [Dakota] and Bean [Carson] in, give them hugs and kisses from me. Go outside look at the stars and count them. Don't forget to smile.

Love always,
Your husband
Jess

The meaning embedded in this letter needs no comment or analysis. And the fact that Jesse Givens created a healing legacy for his family is, in its own right, lesson enough for all.

The Last Will and Testament: Then and Now

The last will and testament remains the most common form of "final words" in developed societies. This legal document bequeaths material possessions from one person to another, usually from one generation to the next. In the United States, preparation of the last will and testament typically involves a document drawn up by an attorney that is witnessed, notarized, and signed by the testator/testatrix. This legal document gives directives for the disposition of property, wealth, and assets. Over the centuries, men wrote legal testaments to their male children and relatives. It wasn't until after suffrage that women were legally permitted to own property and then to bequeath inheritances.

The businesslike last will and testament and its various codicils have come to represent our final good-byes. But in earlier times the character of the last will and testament was broader and deeper. I randomly reviewed a dozen wills from the eighteenth and nineteenth centuries in the United States. Though written with the technical language of the time, there was also a decidedly more personal tone to these documents. Some of them included specific messages to loved ones, as evidenced in the following will of Henry Potter that was written in 1854:

> Knowing the instability of all human affairs the uncertain tenure of life and the certainty of death I wish to set my house

in order; and to prepare for my departure, so this and I make this my last will and testament, this Twenty ninth day of October, A.D. 1853. I commend my spirit to him who gave it, hoping through this merit and all sufficiency of the blessed savior that my sins may be blotted out, that my heart may be purified by the Holy Spirit and that by the unmerited mercy and grace of a sin pardoning God, I may be admitted at last into the new Jerusalem there to join the heavenly host in praise and adoration to God and the Lamb forever. What little worldly substances I may possess I give it all to my dear daughter Mary Ann Potter with full power to use or dispose of the house as she may think proper without rendering an inventory or account of sales.- the paying the debts I may owe in the Town of Fayetteville if there be a sufficiency and I appoint my said daughter, Mary Ann my sole Executor of this my last Will and Testament which I shall deposit with my most valuable papers, and which is written, signed & sealed with my own hand, this day of the date -

H. Potter

Seal

But for the facility of Probate, I now on this sixteenth day of March 1854, I acknowledge the above to be my hand & seal, act & deed, and I here by declare & publish the same to be my last Will & Testament in the presence of - S. L. Hawley

H. Potter

Seal[16]

As evident in this nineteenth-century last will and testament, there is a bequeathing of material possessions, but the heart of it is a personal narrative. This stands in great contrast to contemporary wills. My own current will is eight pages long and has seven articles or sections. After surveying a number of formats for legal wills, I compiled a list of sections that can be found in contemporary wills:

> Identification of testator/testatrix; Revocation; Identification of family; Disinheritance; Executors; Payment of debts; Payment of taxes; Property to trustee; Distribution of property; Special gifts; Debts, expenses, and taxes; Residue and alternate residue; Payments and holding for minors; Trusts; Power to sell or hold; Powers of the executor; Investments; Payments of charities; Distribution in kind; Real estate; Settlement of claims; Exculpatory provision; Professional advisor; Agency; Exoneration; Limiting interest of spouses of beneficiaries; Trustee or executor compensation; Guardians of children; Noncontestability of bequests; Signature; Notary.

Although every legal will does not include all thirty-one sections, it is safe to say that most contemporary wills contain many of these sections. It would also be accurate to conclude that they are written in formal, legal terminology rather than a personal narrative.

Contrasting old and new wills reveals interesting themes. One of them is that people have developed more complex lives and have amassed more earthly possessions, as seen in the increased length and technicality of the contemporary will. The contrast also indicates a migration from "testament" to "will." By this I refer to the shift in text from a narrative, personal tone to a taking-care-of-business, technical tone. There is dispersion of property and material goods, but there is no attention to relational or emotional inheritance.

How did formal legal wills become the main rudder of our death preparation? Why does it remain so? The answer to the first question may be linked to the beginnings of land ownership. The answer to the second is likely more complex. As discussed in upcoming chapters, death has become more invisible in developed countries. When this invisibility is added to psychological death denial, we begin turning away from more painful—and intimate—aspects of death. The evolution from a personal sharing to the dispersion of property in legal wills merits further study. Ultimately, what has been lost in the migration process is a *presence of voice*. And along with that, we have lost a fuller sense of honoring relationships and providing a final good-bye and a healing legacy.

Beyond the Last Will and Testament

The concept of writing Final Words is an original idea that grew from events surrounding my father's sudden death and past correspondences that I serendipitously discovered. This seed found fertile soil as I began reflecting upon the sudden deaths on September 11, 2001, ongoing terrorist threats and attacks around the world, and being a parent. So one day I sat down at my computer and wrote letters of good-bye to my family—in case of my sudden death. I later came to name these "Final Words" and shortly afterward began writing *Nothing Left Unsaid*. At the time I was unaware of ethical wills. When I discovered them about a year later, I was thrilled that such an idea could be considered valuable.

The spirit of Final Words overlaps with hospice legacies,

ethical wills, and wartime letters while maintaining a unique process and identity of its own. Though all of these forms of communication can function as a historical legacy or personal memoir, Final Words are intended to be a healing legacy that honors the *relationship* between people. For it is within this context that healing is generated. Another difference is that Final Words are written when we are well, if there is ample opportunity for the writer to tend to relationships and work through conflicts in the here and now. Additionally, the direct expression of love, forgiveness, and farewell is encouraged. Rather than being a memorial about the person who died, Final Words are a healing legacy for loved ones who survive.

Having reviewed various rituals for final messages, it is important to state that it doesn't matter which form we choose, as long as we ensure our loved ones have final good-byes from us.

Paying It Forward

If you decide to create a healing legacy for your loved ones by writing final messages, and they do so in turn for their loved ones, then your one initial blessing could continue exponentially. A friend commented on how a similar idea was expressed in a movie. In *Pay It Forward,* written by Leslie Dixon, a young boy thinks the world could change for the better if one person did favors for three people, who in turn did favors for three other people. Viewed in this way, the boy's lovely (though fictional) plan was literally exponential. Writing final messages is not the same thing as doing someone a favor, but the possibility that healing might spread through this new ritual is not lost on me.

The following words from Dr. Ira Byock's wonderful book, *Dying Well: Peace and Possibilities at the End of Life,* reveal how healing can happen when nothing is left unsaid: "Progressive terminal illness, in contrast to sudden death, offers a chance to reconcile strained relationships or to complete relationships. Completion does not require ending interaction or severing a relationship; rather, it means that there is nothing left unsaid or undone . . . the history of a relationship and family is transformed when the story of two persons ends well."[17]

All of our stories can end well. We need to be writing Final Words and Legacy Letters now since no one knows when anyone will die. And although various services exist for writing legal wills, there isn't an accessible guide for people of all ages and denominations who wish to write personal, final messages. I hope this book will serve as a guide to help you create healing legacies for your progeny and friends. For we are progressing toward our own death, without our consent or awareness, all the time.

If the mere thought of death gets in the way of writing final messages, it can help to stand on the shoulders of giants. Thich Nhat Hahn, an internationally respected Zen master, encourages us to embrace the relationship between life and death. He teaches that life and death are but two faces of one reality, and that once we realize this, we will have the courage to encounter both. "We must look death in the face, recognize and accept it, just as we look at and accept life."[18]

From this perspective, writing Final Words and Legacy Letters is not only about facing death, it is also about facing life. And that is definitely something to pay forward.

CHAPTER 2

MOVING BEYOND RESISTANCE
TO BENEFITS

IT IS DIFFICULT to begin writing final messages. Whether it is Final Words that will be read by a loved one after we die or a Legacy Letter read by a loved one who may die, we all face some type of resistance. The difficulty may be due to the fact that it's just too difficult to think about death. Or perhaps it's because of practical matters such as not knowing what to say or not having enough time. These reasons are natural and normal. But if you become very still and reflect on the idea of writing final messages, you will confront the reality that you are the only one who can give away your legacy to your parents, your children, and your other loved ones.

Knowing how instrumental you are may still not be reason enough to write. But that's all right, because another motivation exists: creating a healing legacy also benefits the writer. Although the ultimate product of Final Words is to help heal the grief of those whom we leave behind, and the ultimate product of a Legacy Letter is to honor the life of a person who is likely to pass before you, the first time you write a final message, you may discover how good it is for *you*. There are many possible benefits. Writing allows people to reflect upon—and perhaps improve—current lives and relationships. It may bring renewed energy to worn-out issues. Writing can also help clarify purpose and bring more meaning to daily life. In fact, there is discussion within the hospice field about how to more intentionally increase the meaning of life through death awareness. Dr. John Mueller, medical director of Bon Secours Hospice in Richmond, Virginia, refers to this as "finding meaning in living and dying."[1] Holding the tension between life and death—and finding meaning there—is a familiar experience for hospice workers. The ritual of writing Final Words and Legacy Letters allows us all to hold that tension and find meaning there.

You may be wondering, *What if I don't have renewed energy after I write? Or what if I feel worse? How will I recognize whether my relationships have improved? What if my purpose in life is just as unfocused as ever?* These are important and valid questions. And there are many different answers, which I do not pretend to have. But I can expose some resistance that may get in the way, as well as specific solutions.

Writing final good-byes requires introspection and reflection. But the multitasking nature of technology in many industrialized countries does not provide much practice—or time—for looking inside ourselves. We are distracted by a constant stream of information that gushes from our cell phones, e-mails, television, and newspaper. And this doesn't even include the ever-growing daily to-do list and meetings or appointments. In addition to this outer commotion, distractions may also originate from inside to get in the way of reflection. Yet such inner distractions may simply be serving as *messengers*. We may not like the intensity or form of the message (anxiety, physical pain, addiction), but sometimes it must be extreme to get our attention. Stephen Gilligan, an internationally respected psychologist and trainer, suggests that our symptoms are generated by the unconscious and have a positive intent.[2] Thus the message beneath the symptom may ultimately be about healing. And if we pay attention to our resistance to writing final messages, we may find healing for ourselves (as well as for our loved ones).

Benefits for the Writer

The most immediate benefit of writing final messages is a sense of satisfaction in knowing that your final messages to loved ones have been taken care of. But there can be so much more.

When you sit down to write Final Words or Legacy Letters, apart from staring into the unknown abyss of death, you are essentially reflecting on your relationship with the person to whom you are writing. And you are doing this without anyone telling you what to say or how to say it. No one is judging you. It can feel as freeing as journal writing. But then you begin to realize that you're not writing in a journal and it isn't just any letter. As you continue writing, you see what other people's lives will be like without you. Your perspective changes when you start to look at life in this way. I refer to this experience as the *eternity perspective*. It may seem odd or uncomfortable to think about, but this perception actually trumps death denial and fear. And this is a very good thing.

You will also notice negative feelings begin to fade as you continue writing final messages. In place of these negative feelings, or perhaps right alongside them, you may begin to notice other experiences such as being realistic, courageous, honest, and generous. After you complete and review your final messages, you may experience a sense of cleansing. Perhaps even redemption.

You will likely discover other benefits to writing Final Words and Legacy Letters. I continue to learn how the writing process has the power to reveal the unexpected. And since Final Words and Legacy Letters are written when you and your loved ones are alive, you still have the opportunity to address or change what may come up. The writing process may prompt you to improve a relationship or begin a long overdue discussion. Or perhaps it may move you to write a Legacy Letter so your loved ones don't have to wait until you are gone to know the positive feelings you have for them.

Renewed Energy

A sense of renewed energy can develop after writing Final Words and Legacy Letters. I think of this renewed energy as being a by-product, since it is not the intended goal. We typically think about our death or the death of a loved one as solely negative. And although someone's death may result in our feelings of loss, grief, sadness, guilt, or fear, we may also experience positive feelings as we reflect upon the life of the deceased person. Similarly, the writing process is not solely negative.

The sense of positive or renewed energy associated with writing final messages can be compared to the way people feel after a near-death experience or after recovering from a potentially terminal illness. As a result of this brush with death, people may recommit to live life differently—and better. You may know someone who has experienced a near-death experience, or you may have experienced one yourself. Talking with such people often reveals their joyful sense of purpose—and presence. It might be a radiant glow just beneath the surface. Or it could be the way they look you directly in the eye with extraordinary openness.

When I wrote Final Words to my family, renewed energy came to me in the form of calmness rather than a joie de vivre. And I liked it. Not only because I felt a sense of peace knowing that if I suddenly died, my loved ones would receive a legacy that might help their healing, but also because I caught a glimpse of what my life was about—or rather what it should be about. I took inventory of my personal failures and satisfactions, and I gained clarity about how I wanted to be with my family and friends. Mostly this involved being fully present when I was with them, revealing more about myself (the good and the bad), and not becoming stressed over small things. I began letting go of slights and barbs sooner (I highly recommend this). I also found more direction about the next stage of my career. The whole process was like finding a compass that said, *Go this way, Mary.*

Clarifying Purpose and Increasing Meaning

The topic of clarifying life's purpose merits volumes. The popularity of Rick Warren's *The Purpose Driven Life: What on Earth Am I Here For?* verifies the importance of clarifying purpose and finding meaning in people's lives.[3] Warren's book is based in Christian tradition, so its popularity also suggests that people are looking to God for their guidance. Writing Final Words and Legacy Letters may be most healing when we are open to or actively seeking a divine source to guide us. It can also serve as a form of prayer if it brings people closer to their God. But prayer is not necessary for writing final messages. Perhaps words of love are graced no matter what we do.

The eternity perspective that we gain when writing final messages allows us to view what is petty as small and what is important as a priority. This idea is not new. Charles Dickens's *A Christmas Carol* is a classic example of how looking back on our lives from eternity can help us reevaluate our daily decisions and relationships. I encourage you to consider reading more comprehensively about the broader topic of clarifying life's purpose. Writing final messages may help you clarify many aspects of your life. This illumination, in turn, will likely aid the writing process.

Healing Relationships

Honoring relationships so that our loved ones will have closure and a personal legacy is a life purpose in its own right. It is important, perhaps even sacred, work. The concept of writing Final Words and Legacy Letters is rooted in the belief that relationships can be both healing and healed. And the relationship we have with ourselves is central to the relationships we develop with others. Whether we are demanding or nurturing, forgiving or bitter, kind or berating, is often connected to how we relate to ourselves. Not surprisingly, this self-relationship often results from how others treated us in early relationships, as well as how people currently interact with us. Another way to conceptualize this collection of relationships within ourselves is, *Every "I" is a "we."* [4] The self is plural; it is the total of all the people who have affected our lives. We are relational sponges and we absorb our very selves along the way.

Below is a list of questions that can help you reflect on current and past relationships and how the two are intertwined. It is my hope that this reflection will not only aid your writing, but will also directly benefit you. Read the questions. Write or say your answers out loud. Let the process become a source of meditation, thanksgiving, or prayer:

- Who are the people in your life who believed in you and loved you? Who are the people in your life who you believe in and love?
- Who or what helps you be kind and nurturing with yourself? With others?
- What do you fear most? How does this affect your relationship with others?
- What positive personal characteristics do others admire in you? How do you share these in your daily life . . . at work, school, or with family?
- How have you made this world a better place in your daily life with friends and family? In your community? Beyond?

- What gets in the way of being your best self when you are alone? With others?

If none of the information in this section has helped you begin to clarify yourself in relation to others, the distance provided by allegories in books, plays, and movies may be of assistance. Any of these can help untangle an inner struggle or allow an unnoticed blessing to surface. In F. Scott Fitzgerald's classic book *The Great Gatsby,* readers recognize what perpetuates Jay's untouchable loneliness. In John Steinbeck's *East of Eden*, we are inspired by Aaron's forgiveness of Kate and Caleb. And in Frank Capra's *It's a Wonderful Life*, we count the times that angels earn wings while rooting for a troubled man to find his way back home. In parallel fashion, at some unconscious level within, each of us is simultaneously figuring all of this out for ourselves.

Many other venues provide opportunities for us to consider how to be in right relationship with self and others. But it seems there is a strong link between clarifying life purpose and being in right relationship with self and others. When we make this connection, our lives become bent toward health and healing. And this can help us be in a better place from which to write final messages.

Helping Marriages

One exercise in marital therapy workshops involves having couples write the following to their spouse or partner: *"Things I want you to know in case I am not here . . ."* This exercise is similar to writing (and reading) real Final Words. And it can be very powerful. This was the case for Micah and Ellen, who sought marriage counseling to recover from Micah's recent affair. He had experienced a depression in response to a business failure, and instead of reaching out to his wife, he had an affair. Ellen was so hurt and angry, and Micah was so afraid he had already lost her, that neither could see they still loved each other.

This is how marriages can die. The original light of love is blanketed by layers of disappointment, betrayal, depression, or just the daily grind. It becomes difficult for any light to shine through this darkness. And that doesn't even take into consideration the hidden parts of ourselves that we tuck away into our psychological shadow. Abandonment and rejection fears hide inside of us until we show them the way out. For Micah's part, the introspection process of writing final messages to the wife he had just betrayed helped him connect with healthy shame *(I did something wrong)* and lessen the toxic shame he had been defending against *(I am a failure; there is something wrong with me)*. Bringing this into awareness allowed Micah to verbalize the apologies that a betrayed spouse needs to hear after an affair, sometimes for years. Countless reminders pop up after an affair to trigger hurt in the one who was betrayed. But when betrayers are filled with toxic shame, they are more likely to withdraw. As if injured by the hurt spouse's anger and mistrust, they refrain from offering the balm of empathy and continual apology.

And how did writing Final Words help Ellen? She had to face the necessary decision about forgiving her husband's hurtful betrayal. When current or past hurts are viewed from an eternity perspective, the power to condemn or free others becomes penetratingly evident. Writing final messages to Micah was the beginning of Ellen's decision to forgive him.

Overall, this couple's journey back to each other suggests that the mere act of reflecting on our lives and relationships from an eternity perspective can allow us to make positive changes in relationships *now.* This is especially true when we approach the writing of Final Words and Legacy Letters with an open heart and clear mind. And perhaps as this story suggests, approaching it as a part of marital reconciliation.

Renewed energy, peacefulness, clarifying purpose, increasing meaning, and improving relationships are some of the benefits for writers. Each of you will likely find your own treasure in writing final messages—at least that's my hope for you.

Overcoming Inner Resistance: You and Your Shadow

In its simplest form, the term *shadow* refers to the things we don't readily see or know about ourselves. *Shadow projection* can be described as overgeneralizing something we learned in the past and that we (inaccurately) apply to current situations and people. I hope the following information illustrates how shadow can get in the way of writing final messages and ultimately prevent people from experiencing the benefits of writing.

The reasons that we experience difficulty writing final messages will vary. I begin with interpersonal conflict, since relationships are at the heart of writing final messages. Given the ubiquitous nature of relationships in our lives, it makes sense that conflict will arise. But people can be quick to identify what the *other* person has done and focus on how the *other* person's temperament or lifestyle is not acceptable. These reasons may or may not be valid. But when an interpersonal conflict becomes entrenched, it may have more to do with *us* than with the other person. This is where shadow comes into play.

Shadow is a psychological construct purported to exist in an individual's unconscious mind. Shadow represents a hidden place where we involuntarily tuck away the things we don't readily see or want to know about ourselves. In the preceding situation, Micah unconsciously tucked away the vulnerable parts of himself into his shadow. According to Jungian theory, our shadow parts can be both negative and positive. And though hidden from us, they may be readily visible to others. An integrated awareness of what we unconsciously hide away in our shadows is needed to complete our wholeness as spiritual and human beings. Bringing shadow into awareness, or "shadow work," is considered necessary by many psychotherapists. It was certainly an important part of healing Micah and his marriage relationship. This concept may seem abstract or complex, but please bear with me, because our shadows can negatively affect how we write our final messages—including whether we write them at all.

What is shadow work and how is it done? A beginning step is to recognize our shadow parts. Since they are so well hidden, sometimes we have to look for them indirectly. We can pay attention to physical or psychological symptoms. We can also look at a strong interpersonal conflict we have with someone. Many of these behaviors and symptoms can, of course, have different causes. But if shadow is involved, it can be reassuring to know that if we shine a light inside and see what's there (as Micah did), we can begin to reclaim our wholeness and improve important relationships.

Shadow Projection and Writing

When interpersonal conflict makes it difficult to write final messages to certain people, shadow work can be helpful. And reflective writing is one way to do this work. More specifically, writing may allow us to identify our "projections," which can be described as the psychological process of creating an image or expectation in our mind—often one that is based on a past experience—and acting as though it is happening in the present. It's almost as if the person we are currently relating to is a blank movie screen upon which we "project" our own scenes. As you can imagine, projection negatively affects relationships, because it makes it difficult to see who and what is *really* there. For example, Micah did not share his vulnerability with his wife, because he did not think he could trust her. But his lack of trust had nothing to do with Ellen. An earlier rupture in Micah's development of trust was unfairly being projected onto Ellen. A different example involves the mother who never grieved the loss of her father as a teenager and cannot recognize her own teen's struggle with losses.

Past hurts, feelings of shame, and stalwart defenses can create multilayered filters that distort our present relationships and interactions. Psychotherapists from Freud and Jung to present-day therapists tell us that all of this happens on an unconscious level—and it happens quite often. Indeed, being truly present in a relationship involves not only seeing what is there, but also *not* seeing what is *not* there. Writing Final Words and Legacy Letters are relational tasks, and our shadows can distort relationships when we do not see the other person as they truly are. As we sit down to write final messages, shadow energy can pop out in the form of anger, resentment, bitterness, or other negative emotions toward the other person. An unseen army of past experiences (fears, hurts, regrets) may march through our mind and lead us to lose sight of the real person, who, like us, is just doing the best they can.

One way to address an interpersonal conflict is to take back some of the projections we inaccurately—and unknowingly—cast upon others. To get traction and move beyond both projection and conflict, reflect on the questions below. I suggest writing out the answers, rather than just thinking about them, to better expose shadow:

- Why do I feel so much resentment toward this person? When have I experienced similar feelings early in my life? Later in life?
- Why do I feel such anger toward this person? Who else have I felt this angry toward early in my life? At other times?
- Why do I feel so betrayed by this person? When have I felt betrayed like this before?
- Why do I feel so hurt by this person? Who else has hurt me in this same, deep way?
- Why am I afraid to write to this person? When did I first feel afraid to express my intimate thoughts and feelings?

- Why do I find it so hard to accept this person as he or she is? When was I not accepted by someone important early in life? Late in life?

When these questions are asked and answered honestly, we may begin to recognize some of the shadows that we have projected onto others. After we have done some of this shadow work, we are in a better position to identify what role we need to play in resolving the conflict—perhaps even to heal a wounded relationship. If individual introspection does not help you to identify hidden parts of yourself, then it may be good to explore these questions with a mentor, friend, or therapist. The answers can lead to the source of difficulty. And as suggested, the original source may not even be the person with whom we are currently having difficulty.

Parenting through the Shadows

In Robert Johnson's book *Owning Your Own Shadow,* he tells us that children benefit when parents reclaim their shadows: "If you wish to give your children the best possible gift, the best possible entree into life, remove your shadow from them. To give them a clean heritage, psychologically speaking, is the greatest legacy. And, incidentally, you will go far in your own development by taking your shadow back into your private psychological structure—where it first originated and where it is required for your own wholeness."[5]

Projecting shadow onto children is like overcorrecting a car. We think we're doing the right thing, but we're actually making things worse. Healthy parenting involves seeing children as they truly are and not projecting our own needs, fears, and regrets onto our children. The following example illustrates how writing final messages helped a parent recognize some of her projections and begin to provide welcoming shade instead of harmful shadow.

Carrie was described by others as a "critical" and "controlling" parent. She constantly pushed her daughter to do better. Carrie was unable to see the difference between setting goals and demanding perfection. She had positive conscious intentions for her child, as most parents do. But this desire was filtered through her own unfulfilled life goals and past failures. In other words, she was projecting her shadow onto her daughter. Although she was smart enough, Carrie never went to college. So when she became a parent herself, she was determined that the same thing would not happen to her daughter. That was the conscious part. The unconscious shadow part (the overcorrection) was responsible for the impossible standards she was setting for her daughter.

By the time I met with Carrie's daughter, she was twenty years old, and it was clear that the pressure thrust upon her for so long had finally reached a peak. Carrie's daughter was now having regular panic attacks when she thought about the possibility of not getting an "A" in her first college course. Although a single factor rarely predicts an outcome like this, temperament can indeed play a role in whether someone becomes anxious or easily lets go of a low test grade. But in this situation, the daughter's boundaries had been chronically violated by her mother's perfectionistic shadow. So much so, the daughter's greatest fear was letting her mother down, rather than not reaching her own goals. Carrie's shadow projection had blotted out her daughter's very self.

Now consider what it would be like for this daughter to receive the following Legacy Letter. Carrie actually wrote Final Words first, which revealed some shadow behavior to her. And since she wanted the healing to start sooner rather than later, Carrie decided to write the following Legacy Letter both to celebrate her daughter and to initiate reconciliation:

Dearest Daughter,

I have always been proud of you for who you are and for how hard you have worked. I realize now that setting such a "high bar" with your academics is negatively affecting you. I want you to know that I am very sorry for hurting you in this way. I never intended this to happen; I just wanted you to have a better life than I did. When my parents didn't send me to college, I was hurt and ashamed. I never wanted that to happen to you. The truth is, I felt like I never measured up to my parents and, ironically, I have created the same experience for you. I love you very much and hope that as you make friends and choose boyfriends, you will find people who like you for who you are, not how well you perform. I love you just the way you are—you don't have to be perfect for me or anyone else.

Love always,
Mom

You can probably imagine the range of emotions that Carrie's daughter felt after receiving this letter: confusion, joy, anger, and forgiveness (to name a few). One immediate outcome was improvement in the mother-daughter relationship. Another was that Carrie became more able to see her daughter as she really was—and not how Carrie needed her to be. A final benefit was for Carrie. The unflinching honesty she developed allowed her to feel freer with herself than she had ever felt before.

Unless we do conscious work on shadow, it is almost always projected. Therapy can help us discover and integrate shadow. We can also journal, meditate, pray, or read (Robert Johnson's book is a good resource—see page 50). And perhaps the process of writing final messages can also serve to help people recognize and begin to integrate shadow.

Grief Connections

In addition to shadow interference, unresolved grief from previous deaths or losses can negatively affect writing final messages. People may first discover this when they sit down to write. They may also discover it in the *resistance* to sitting down to write. As death and grief educator Harold Ivan Smith suggests, grief from previous losses can get "re-booted" when people come into contact with new losses or anticipatory grief. [6] Revisiting earlier unresolved grief or loss can work together for our good, though, because it provides us with another opportunity to grieve—and perhaps to heal.

I often describe grief as a door that people must eventually pass through so they can get to the other side of their loss. The passage is not supposed to be hurried—or ignored. Going through the door doesn't mean that sadness will leave and everything will be better, or that the person who died will be betrayed or forgotten. Rather, going through the door means feeling what you feel when you feel it. And it must be done. While this explanation sounds simple, the grief journey is far from simple. Grief elicits different images and experiences for different people. Some of the experiences people report include sadness, loneliness, anger, confusion, guilt, and loss. Though these are familiar emotions, they can take on visceral weight when associated with grief. It is also important to recognize that not all emotions associated with the death of a loved one are negative. Some people can experience gratitude, relief, and transcendent meaning in life.

The pioneer Elisabeth Kubler-Ross brought much-needed dialogue and attention to grief and death.[7] She is noted for identifying five stages of the grief process: denial, anger, bargaining, depression, and acceptance. True "staging" is rare in human development, so although Kubler-Ross's stages are listed in succession, please know that people may not experience all of these feelings and that they can be experienced out of sequence. Indeed, people often experience grief in an unpredictable way, going back and forth through these stages for months and years—sometimes even within the same day. The only known constant regarding grief is that everyone's process is unique and there is no predictable timetable. Many excellent books exist to help people adjust after loss and manage their grief after a sudden or expected death. [8, 9, 10]

Complicated and Unresolved Grief

Acute distress is normal following the loss of a loved one. But when grief reactions reach extreme physical or psychological intensity and duration, they can interfere with daily functioning. This is often referred to as *complicated or unresolved grief.* The reaction I had after my father's sudden death seemed normal at first (whatever "normal" is), but then it became complicated. I could function at work and home, but I experienced less enjoyment in life. At times, I also still had remnants of that heavy sensation in my body. My complicated grief reaction was relatively mild, and it was related to the traumatic nature of experiencing the sudden death of a loved one. Over time it got better, and finding the letters my father and I had exchanged was part of this healing.

Other people, whose complex grief reactions are more severe, can experience interference in their daily functioning for a long period of time. And it isn't uncommon for physical illnesses to follow. There is considerable clinical interest in complicated grief as being distinct from major depression, panic disorder, and posttraumatic stress disorder (PTSD), and there is debate about whether complicated grief is a valid diagnosis or definition. When normal grief reactions become complicated, it may also be the result of PTSD.[11,12] In general, though, grief reactions are affected by circumstances surrounding the death, such as whether it resulted from violence and whether it was sudden or expected. The age of death (child or young adult versus elderly) can also affect the grieving process.

All of this information suggests that the loss associated with grief is a multidimensional construct. Yet one dimension lies at the core of grief recovery: people cannot fully grieve alone. Our grief must be witnessed, legitimized, and comforted by a caring other. We cannot go through that grief door alone. So if you feel any resistance to writing your Final Words or a Legacy Letter, it may be helpful to do a "loss history."[13] Look back on your life through the lens of grief, keeping in mind that grief can result from losses other than death, including divorce, relocation, house fires, and other such traumas. If you think that unresolved loss issues are affecting you, then grief recovery work may be helpful. This can take the form of a face-to-face talk with a trusted friend, spiritual mentor, or professional counselor. It could also include reflection through journaling or attending local grief workshops offered in your area. Further information and resources for coping with grief can be found on the Web site Griefnet.com, one of the largest online supports for the bereaved.

Don't let unresolved grief and loss get in the way of writing final messages to loved ones. And keep in mind that your Final Words will likely provide much needed comfort for their grief when you are gone.

Did They Know?

Lingering questions can haunt the bereaved—especially if a sudden death occurred. *Did Mom love me? Did she approve of my decisions? Did she know I forgave her? Did Dad know how much I loved him? Did he really accept me? Was he proud of me? Did Bob know that I respected him despite our differences? Did Grandpa know how grateful I was?*

When these questions remain unanswered, they can become a source of guilt, complicated grief, unresolved loss, or all three. Each of us can have difficulty expressing intimate thoughts and feelings to a loved one or significant person at some point in our lives. Such difficulty can prevent us from saying what most needs to be said—or heard. We may also delay saying something important because it is assumed there will always be another opportunity to do so. But each of us has the opportunity to make sure that our loved ones hear what they most need to know by writing final messages. Answering these questions can help comfort this aspect of grief.

Final messages also comfort the grief of a loved one when it evokes feelings of gratitude. Indeed, people who receive and read final messages report feeling grateful for the unique messages they received as well as for the concrete reminder of the relationship they shared with the deceased. Though such memories bring sadness, integrating gratitude into the grief experience can help facilitate healing.[14]

The Role of Temperament and Personality

Temperament and personality can also affect how—or if—we express intimate thoughts and feelings. Final Words and Legacy Letters represent some of our most vulnerable, honest, and joyful thoughts and feelings. Not all of us are equally adept at this type of emotional expression, for a variety of reasons. Temperament and personality are two of these reasons. And since they cut across gender, sex, race, ethnicity, culture, and class lines to affect emotional expression, these two aspects merit a closer look.

The word "temperament" is typically used to describe children's stylistic behavioral tendencies, while "personality" is used to describe similar and more permanent traits in adults.

Temperament involves both physiological and psychological components. Most theorists and researchers recognize there is a strong genetic predisposition toward particular temperaments, such as shyness, moodiness, and anxiousness. This genetic component makes it particularly difficult for people to "change their stripes." Yet sometimes knowledge about temperament helps us understand and adapt. Alice Shannon, a parent and therapist, describes how her "difficult" child was no longer a frustrating puzzle after discovering how temperament influences the way children respond to the world around them.[15]

I often think of personality as "grown up" temperament. John Mayer provides a more scholarly definition: "Personality is the organized developing system within the individual that represents the collective action of . . . motivational, emotional, cognitive, social-planning, and other psychological subsystems."[16] Personality research often focuses on trait identification. A popular personality assessment, the Myers-Briggs Type Indicator (MBTI), helps people understand their processing and interactional styles. Information from this instrument yields dominant personality traits along four dimensions: introversion/extroversion; intuitive/sensing; thinking/feeling; and perceiving/judging.[17] Robert McCrae and Paul Costa have also conducted extensive research on adult personality, resulting in the Big Five trait clusters of neuroticism, extroversion, openness to experiences, agreeableness, and conscientiousness.[18]

How might temperament and personality directly affect writing final messages? First, it is important to keep in mind that while it is difficult to change our stripes, biology is not destiny. Next, let's pull together personality information from the Big Five and MBTI and consider a hypothetical person who is sensitive, open to experiences, conscientious, feeling, and introverted. It is easy to see how these traits in a person would likely translate to a natural ease with emotional expression —and also with writing Final Words or Legacy Letters. Another example of how personality can influence writing is evident in people's choice of careers. Using MBTI language, people in the engineering profession tend to be more *thinking than feeling,* while people in the human services professions (counseling, social work) tend to be more *feeling than thinking.* Thus, the engineer may write a brief and pithy final message, and the social worker may write pages. Neither is better; they simply reflect the writer's personality.

Building upon these two examples, it simply helps when we know ourselves. Indeed, *know thyself* has been an imperative to humans since the Oracle at Delphi in ancient Greece. From a more contemporary perspective, it naturally follows that based on our temperament and personality, some of us will feel more comfortable than others as we craft important and intimate messages to our loved ones. But just because something doesn't feel natural does not mean that it cannot be done. Think about the first time you tried to ride a bike, roller skate, or dribble a soccer ball. You get better at it once you get over your initial difficulties.

So our Final Words and Legacy Letters will ultimately reflect our personalities. And surely our strengths and weaknesses, our quirks and endearing traits, will come through. We will all likely find ourselves needing to stretch a little to express that which is necessary but does not come naturally. Since there is no such thing as "the perfect final message," we must instead strive to write in a way that reflects our true selves and that honors the people in our lives. This is all any of our loved ones will expect from us—and us from them.

Making a Real Difference

If someone you love has already died, you might be thinking that there is nothing you can do to make a difference. The truth is that although you can no longer directly affect that person's life, certain rituals may help you and other loved ones transcend his or her death. Described more fully in the next chapter, "Remembering Practices" is an idea developed by Lorraine Hedtke that involves maintaining connections by telling and writing stories about the person who has died.[19] You can probably imagine how such stories serve to honor the deceased while promoting a healthy connection for survivors.

In some ways, the following story is an example of a Remembering Practice, Final Words, and a Legacy Letter all rolled into one. It is also an example of how writing—indeed words—make a difference. Published in the wonderful book *Small Miracles,* by Yitta Halberstam and Judith Levanthal, it is the story of Adam Riklis and his son, Joey Riklis.[20] The two men became estranged when Joey decided to travel instead of attending college. The elder Mr. Riklis was a holocaust survivor who had worked his entire life to give Joey the privileges he and his family had never experienced. Attending college was one of these, so he was disappointed when Joey chose travel over an advanced education. Joey and his father were unable to reconcile before Mr. Riklis died. In fact, Joey didn't learn about his father's heart attack and subsequent death until he ran into a friend from high school while he was traveling. Joey felt sad and responsible for his father's death; he also felt a calling back to his family's religion. So he flew to Israel and immediately went to Jerusalem's Wailing Wall. The following excerpt tells what took place there:

"Oh, Dad," he sobbed. "How I wish I could ask your forgiveness! How I wish I could tell you how much I loved you! How much I regret all the pain I caused you! I didn't mean to hurt you, Dad. I was just trying to find my own way. You meant everything to me, Dad. I wish I could tell you that."

When Joey finished praying, he turned around, at a loss at what to do next. Then he observed people around him scribbling notes and inserting them into the crevices of the Wall. Curious as to what this behavior meant, he approached a young man, and asked, "Excuse me, why are so many people putting little pieces of paper into the cracks of the Wall?"

"Oh, these are their petitions," the youth answered, "their prayers. It is believed that the stones are so holy that requests placed inside of them will be especially blessed."

"Can I do that, too?" Joey asked, intrigued.

"Sure. But be warned, it isn't easy to find an empty crevice anymore!" the young man laughed. "Jews have been coming here for centuries to ply God with their prayers!"

Joey wrote: "Dear Father, I beg you to forgive me for the pain I caused you. I loved you very much and I will never forget you.

And please know that nothing that you taught me was in vain. I will not betray your family's deaths. I promise."

When he had finished writing the note, Joey searched for an empty crevice. The young man had not exaggerated. All of the Wall's cracks were filled, crammed, overflowing with petitioners' notes, and it took him close to an hour to find an empty space. But it turned out not to be empty, after all. When he slid his own small note into the crack, he accidentally dislodged another that had already been resting there, and it fell to the ground. "Oh, no, I've pushed out someone's note." . . . [S]uddenly overcome by a tremendous curiosity to read the words of the unknown petitioner, Joey did something uncharacteristically unscrupulous: He rolled open the note to examine its contents. And this is what he read:

"My Dear Son Joey, If you should ever happen to come to Israel and somehow miraculously find this note, this is what I want you to know: I always loved you, even when you hurt me, and I will never stop loving you. You are, and always will be, my beloved son. And Joey, please know that I forgive you for everything, and only hope that you in turn will forgive a foolish old man."

The note was signed "Adam Riklis, Cleveland, Ohio."[21]

I encourage you to read the entire story, because it doesn't end here. While forgiveness almost has a heartbeat in this story, it is about many other things as well—not the least of which is the powerful legacy that can be found in the exchange of the written word. Much like writing Final Words and Legacy Letters.

CHAPTER 3

FINAL GOOD-BYES
ACROSS CULTURES

MOST OF WHAT we know about death is learned rather than instinctive. We acquire knowledge about death through cultural symbols, religion, languages, the arts, and funerary rites. Cultures organize death beliefs and customs to help people develop a coherent view of mortality. One method of conveying this information through cultures involves social norms, or prescribed customs within a culture. It logically follows that social norms can affect our thoughts and behaviors about death and dying. Though adhering to various social norms can promote cohesion among group members, it can also produce narrow views. Such views may become so embedded that people accept them without question. Since our core values and beliefs can be found in culture, I examine various social norms regarding death and dying across different cultures in this chapter.

Death Denial

One social norm regarding death and dying that dominates mainstream United States culture is *denial*.[1,2] People in this country don't want to think or talk about death. So we don't. There are several sources of death denial. Michael Kearl, a professor of sociology who specializes in death, suggests that the privatization of death and the institutionalization of dying has created an invisibility surrounding the end of life.[3] This invisibility, in turn, has contributed to death denial as becoming a main orientation in the United States.

The hidden nature of death and dying in developed countries may also be related to a lack of living in a community. We don't really know our neighbors anymore. When there is less exposure and connection to community members who die, immediate family members become the primary source of death awareness and education. Yet families are rarely well versed in how to talk about death. As grandparents age, family members may acknowledge death gingerly with statements like, "Grandmother doesn't have many Thanksgivings left, so we should spend it with her this year." These are wonderful ways to begin a conversation about death. But far too often, this is where the dialogue ends. Other common discussions within families focus on the business details of death, such as funeral arrangements and who will inherit certain family heirlooms. But beyond this, there isn't much—if any—emotional death preparation within families.

Death denial can also stem from the simple hope that everyone will live a long life. People typically don't talk about premature death or the possibility of sudden death—and for good reason. Death of any kind is sad and difficult; who *wants* to talk about it? People are also naturally caught up in the busyness of living daily life, and we assume there will be a tomorrow. We take for granted there will always be another opportunity to say what needs to be said to one another.

Another norm surrounding death is the desire not to die alone. Sherwin Nuland, a physician and author of *How We Die,* states, "A promise we [doctors] can keep and a hope we can give is the certainty that no man or woman will be left to die alone."[4] Making sure that loved ones aren't alone when they die prevents one aspect of solitary death. But dying alone doesn't necessarily refer to being *physically* alone. There is a spiritual aloneness that the dying experience when we avoid talking about death with them. Because of our own death denial, depersonalization of the dying, and resulting tendency not to talk about death, terminally ill people often die a "slow-motion death" or a number of "social mini-deaths" before actually physiologically expiring.[5] To me, waiting to die without being able to talk about it with anyone would seem to be the ultimate type of dying alone.

Given the combination of death denial, fear of dying alone, and the invisibility of death, it is safe to conclude that people would benefit from more education about death preparation. But if we don't receive it in our families and culture, where will we get it? Learning about death beliefs that extend beyond our own social norms can be one part of death education. I also hope that talking about and writing Final Words and Legacy Letters will facilitate more death education and reduce death denial in helpful ways.

Early Death Education Lessons

Until recently, I had not considered why I was comfortable with death as a child. A major reason involved the way my parents showed me that death is a part of life. And they did this in simple, nonintrusive ways. Foremost, they did not let death be invisible. They talked openly about their parents' deaths, and they brought my siblings and me to wakes and funerals of relatives and neighbors. We often attended the gatherings after these services. My parents also taught me about death through modeling. When my father's brother, Ponce, was dying of cancer, my dad often drove an hour to a town just outside of Ithaca to be with him. He did this many weekends and always invited us kids to join him. Sometimes I did.

My uncle Ponce was a husband and busy father of six children; he was also a talented athlete and carpenter. It was grim to watch his once strong, tanned body becoming slowly reduced to gaunt weakness over the course of our visits. But there was something about being near him at the end of his life that felt natural and important. Spending time with my uncle and his family allowed me to witness human courage and kindness. I also experienced how a skinny, awkward kid could do something as ordinary as hold the hand of a dying person and know that it helped. What began emerging back then was the awareness that it was both a privilege and a responsibility to witness death—and then watch life continue.

My first experience with sudden death was also constructive. Elaine Smith was one of the few teachers in our Catholic elementary school who wasn't a nun. I remember her smiling often and looking happy, emitting what I now know as the "radiance of a new bride." Her husband began commuting to night school soon after they were married. Winter roads in the Finger Lakes can be treacherous, and even more so when it's dark. Mrs. Smith decided to ride along because she didn't want her husband driving alone at night. To everyone's shock and sadness, Mr. and Mrs. Smith were killed instantly in a car accident on one of those unforgiving winter roads. This was, of course, tragic for their families and friends. Every sudden death is. But being a romantic preteen, I focused on how neither husband nor wife had to be sad, because they died *together*. If there could ever be a happy ending associated with death, this seemed like one.

Some of these positive childhood lessons could be summed up as: *Take care of the sick and dying. Talk to them. Love them. Death is a part of life; and it's not scary. When and why we die is a mystery. Be happy before you die.* But there can be other early lessons that are not so positive or healthy. These include: *Don't cry, be strong; He/she is just asleep; It's not okay to talk about death (the silence mandate). Death isn't fair.* I'm sure you could add to the positive or negative lessons. Correcting the harmful lessons and increasing the beneficial ones cannot be left to chance. When adults do not receive healthy death education or grief support as children, and if they don't get it in adulthood, they may feel unequipped to explain death to children in healthy ways. This generational lack of death education can become an unending cycle. In addition, traumatic deaths can leave communities and adults in shock, making them feel even more unprepared to render comfort to children or provide the container that can help children reestablish a sense of safety.

For me, additional death lessons came later in life as my parents began aging and talking openly about their own death. They did this by inquiring about who wanted certain family possessions. They also regularly reviewed their important legal papers. My husband often remarked about how openly my parents talked about their death. But looking back, I recall that our discussions weren't intimate. At the time I didn't even consider that my parents might have wanted to talk about approaching the end of their lives in more meaningful ways. There isn't a cultural norm or guide for talking about the emotional aspects of death preparation.

I eventually had emotionally intimate conversations with my mother about her own (in due time) death. Several months after my father died, I was visiting my mother for a long spring weekend. The chemotherapy and cancer cells were still waging a war within her, but she was holding her own day by day. I had the luxury of visiting without my husband and children, which let me "just be a daughter," something I hadn't done since college. We had a great time together. The morning I left, we were eating breakfast together in the kitchen. I asked if there was anything else we needed to talk about. My mother was silent for a moment and extended her hand across the table. I rested mine on top of hers. We gazed into each other's eyes and said so much without saying a word. I have never had such an intimate conversation with anyone.

I can still see her sapphire blue eyes welling up as my own tears spilled over. My mom and I have had many conversations about death since then, but this is the most memorable. I'm so glad I didn't miss that moment.

Why Think about Death Preparation Differently?

We need to be thinking and talking about death differently than we do now—especially in developed countries where death has become invisible. What we are currently doing does not appear to make up for death denial or help us face our fear of death. This adds up to many unfortunate outcomes, including a lack of death preparation. Although hospice patients and their families receive some type of formal death education, most of us go without such preparation. We don't have rituals or guides for talking about our own deaths or the death of loved ones. But there are some new ideas about death and grieving that can help us prepare better for death, or at least give us a frame for talking about it.

Mentioned in the previous chapter, "Remembering Practices" is one of those new ideas. Created by Lorraine Hedtke, a social worker and leader in the field of thanatology (which deals with death and how to cope with the psychological issues surrounding it), this concept relies on using a narrative approach to emphasize the ongoing story of relationships.[6] One of the attractive features of such narratives is that they take the focus away from the finality of death and show us that by telling loving stories, a relationship continues long after the person has died. Hedtke also suggests that by employing the power of story to transcend physical mortality, we promote the "re-membering" of lives and connections. Overall, this approach rejects the assumption that people should complete a process of farewell and letting go in order to progress healthily through the crisis and transition of death.

Famous people and community leaders may have monuments or buildings named after them as a way to continue their story. But the majority of people become disconnected from memory—and thus important relationships—by bowing to the finality of death. Indeed, most prevailing customs echo the idea of "letting go and moving on." It would seem that people could benefit from finding ways to foster and maintain relational connections following death.

Writing to document our lives, loves, hopes, and fears is as old as time. Themes in great literature certainly reflect such a practice. The nature of writing and telling stories is inherently flexible and permanent; perhaps this is why storytelling has been a cornerstone of culture throughout time. Flexibility and permanence, though seemingly paradoxical, are important because they can create new dimensions of relationship with the deceased—even following death. On a more personal level, narratives *keep relationships alive.* From this perspective, grief becomes an evolving and creative opportunity for story development and change, rather than an unpleasant task to be worked through as quickly as possible.[7]

We need rituals that will help us both grieve and move on. Remembering Practices is one way; Final Words and Legacy Letters are others. All three rituals contribute to new and necessary discussions about death and dying.

Death Rituals

Rituals for the dead provide a larger context from which to explore death preparation. Rituals are condensed forms of experiences, tips of icebergs of meanings, and social mechanisms for transformations.[8] According to a comprehensive encyclopedia about worldwide death and dying rituals, every human society meets the death of a member with some type of ritual.[9] The purpose of this universal practice is largely based on the benefit that the ritual brings to the living. Death rituals provide similar benefits in every society. The differences involve the formal acts that are performed between the relationships of the dead, the family, and the community. Variation can also emerge from religious tradition, regional custom, poverty, and climate.

A common type of death ritual involves funerary customs. Patterns across cultures typically involve treatment of the body, purifying the body, public grief expression, having a final resting place, conducting a ritual at the final resting place, and sacrifice.[10] While the general benefits of funerary rites include provision of structure and catharsis of emotion, there are specific benefits as well:[11, 12, 13]

- Providing the last rite of passage for the dead
- Celebrating the life of the dead
- Stimulating recollections of the deceased and helping to validate the deceased person's life
- Allowing participation in memorializing the person who died
- Confirming and reinforcing the reality of the death and separation of the living and the dead

- Assisting in acknowledging and expressing feeling of loss and facilitating mourning
- Providing comfort for the bereaved
- Providing means for the community to give and receive social and spiritual support
- Allowing for public acknowledgment of private grief
- Providing meaning for loss
- Beginning the process of helping the bereaved adjust back into the community
- Helping in the search for meaning
- Reminding the living of their mortality
- Furnishing means and methods for disposing of the body
- Changing the identity of the person from living to dead
- Transforming the bereaved into their new identities

Death rituals and funerary rites can be interpreted in many ways. One theme that emerges is how death customs—and, in particular, funerary rites—formalize the transition from life to death. They provide structure to facilitate the adaptation of the bereaved. Another theme is that detailed procedures within specific rituals vary and reflect the unique beliefs of particular cultures. This may mean accepting the permanent departure of a loved one from this life or restoring the balance upset by the death. In a real sense, then, death rituals help re-create social order. In addition, if a particular culture believes that a spirit or soul lives beyond physical death, then death rituals serve as tools for humankind to transform death from a defeat of life to a stepping stone to another, perhaps even better, place.[14] This creates continuity beyond death itself. Finally, death rituals give the bereaved a public forum to make amends or say "I love you" and "good-bye."

Despite the intended function of death rituals, not everyone may experience them as beneficial. However, most would agree that death rituals are a dramatization of a natural event that provide structured bereavement. Yet death rituals change over time, and the grief process is highly individual. This suggests that additional practices will develop as cultures evolve over time.

Death Preparation Practices in the United States

Though death beliefs and rituals are related to death preparation, emotionally preparing for death involves a different process. To identify the different aspects of death preparation that exist in the United States, I reviewed books, journal articles, and electronic media. I quickly discovered that most information focuses on specific death beliefs and rituals rather than on *death preparation* per se. One increasingly popular type of death preparation is the living will, which will likely serve as a bridge to final messages and healing legacies.

Living Wills

The living will includes advance directives for medical treatment in case a person becomes incapacitated and cannot make medical decisions. It is often written by those in middle age and beyond. This will is used for end-of-life care issues and near-fatal medical conditions that render a person comatose or vegetative. When my husband and I wrote our living wills, we used Aging with Dignity's *Five Wishes* booklet.[15] Making decisions about advance directives can be a difficult task, but this clear guide made it much easier. The first four wishes involve medical directives; options are unambiguous and choices can be readily selected. But when I came to the fifth wish, "My Wish for What I Want My Loved Ones to Know," I stopped and stared at the wording. The fifth wish was essentially "preprinted" Final Words! If you are familiar with this particular living will, writers are directed to cross out anything with which they don't agree. Examples include: *I wish to have my family and friends know that I love them; I wish to be forgiven for the times I have hurt my family, friends, and others; I wish to have my family, friends and others know that I forgive them for when they may have hurt me in my life.*

The first draft of this book was almost complete when I read the *Five Wishes* booklet. I began thinking that the concept of Final Words was redundant with this living will. Perhaps people didn't need a book on this topic, because it already existed in this form. But as I kept staring at the checklist, I finally saw the obvious difference. The fifth wish is a checklist written *for* an individual; Final Words is a narrative letter written *by* an individual. While some people may be more comfortable with the prepared checklist, which is certainly better than no final message at all, a checklist cannot compare to a personally written message addressed to a loved one.

I searched other types of living wills in different states. Most of the examples did not include a section similar to this fifth wish. Because of the inherent value of final personal messages to loved ones, perhaps creators of future living wills will begin including them. Or maybe people will simply begin writing Final Words and keeping these with their living wills.

Hospice Care

Hospice experts provide solid ground to patients and families as the once-familiar landscape of their daily lives gets washed away by the shock of imminent death. Hospice care includes emotional and spiritual support as well as the necessary medical and palliative (symptom-reducing) treatment. Specific treatment for dying patients and their families is described elsewhere. Here the focus is on the history of the hospice movement as a way to examine cultural aspects of death preparation.

Organized care for dying persons and their loved ones began with the hospice movement in the late 1960s. More specifically, it started with one hospice center in the United Kingdom. Currently there are approximately seven thousand hospice centers in seventy countries, roughly three thousand of which are in the United States.[16] Hospices may be part of hospitals or health systems or be independently run; they can be nonprofit or for-profit companies. The first hospice in America opened in 1974 as the Connecticut Hospice and was soon followed by an in-patient hospice at Yale Medical Center and a hospice program in Marin County, California.[17] Four years later, the U.S. Department of Health, Education, and Welfare published a report citing hospice as a viable concept of care for terminally ill people and their families that provides humane care at a reduced cost.[18]

Hospices have evolved from volunteer-based, grassroots

organizations into health care companies with paid staff and credentialed practices. As more people have learned about what hospice offers, they have chosen hospice care for their loved ones or themselves. But the real proliferation of hospice in the United States can be traced to Congress's decision in the early 1980s to create legislation that established Medicare coverage for hospice care. The Medicare Hospice Benefit was made permanent in 1986, and today, most states also provide hospice Medicaid coverage. Currently one in every four Americans who die receive hospice care at the end of life.[19]

Cross-Cultural Death Perspectives

To overcome the fear of death and to optimize life, it is essential to examine the traditions of other cultures as well as personal experiences and coping mechanisms.[20] Since people's understanding of death is socially constructed, cross-cultural comparisons of death and dying can help us understand our own beliefs as well as the beliefs of others. It is important to point out that cultural groups are not homogeneous, and individual variation must always be considered in situations of death, grief, and bereavement. This review is not intended to cover every culture nor all degrees of acculturation within each group. It is intended to simply provide a broader perspective for discussing and exploring death preparation rituals.

As our knowledge of death beliefs and dying practices increases, our understanding of human behavior can also expand. This is important for many reasons, as the following true story reveals. There is a Pan-African belief that spirits of the dead remain close to the living soon after death. Knowing about this would have greatly helped personnel in one particular school in the southeastern United States when a boy from Uganda was mainstreamed into a second grade classroom there. An in-depth cultural orientation was not conducted for the boy or his classmates. This is common for most busy public schools. When the boy's grandmother died soon after he arrived in this country, he continued to talk to her both at school and at home—since she was nearby, according to the death beliefs of his culture. Although his family understood this (they were talking with her, too), school personnel thought the boy was suffering from psychosis or complicated grief reactions. Once the family's culture was understood, the "problem" was solved. And the boy's classmates gained a cross-cultural death lesson.

The concept of writing Final Words has to do with facing our mortality when we are alive and well rather than when we are preparing for an eminent death. Yet information about death preparation resides primarily within the death and dying literature—that is, end-of-life rituals and customs. More specifically, it is found within religious traditions, a valuable source of information, since most ethnic groups draw from religious tradition to create cultural customs and understanding. The first part of this cross-cultural review provides an overview of death rituals as practiced by major world religions.

Death Beliefs of Major World Religions

Beliefs about death provide a bridge between death preparation and death rituals. One could argue that most beliefs about death and dying originate from religion. Thus, world religions can provide one way to learn more about death preparation rituals. The following summary, condensed from various sources, indicates that specific practices differ, as do core beliefs and philosophies about death.[21, 22, 23]

Buddhism. Death is part of an ongoing process of reincarnation until a person receives enlightenment. After the physical body dies, the deceased goes through a transformation that may result in rebirth. Buddhists cremate bodies of their dead, and the first seven days after death are the most important for final prayers. During a forty-seven-day mourning period, prayers of the mourners help the deceased's post-death transformation and awaken his or her spirit to the true nature of death. The funeral ritual is vitally important because it ensures safe passage of the deceased into the afterlife.

Christianity. There are many different sects including, but not limited to, Catholicism, Eastern Orthodox, Greek Orthodox, Protestant, Lutheran, Methodist, Baptist, Episcopal, and Presbyterian. Each religion has variations of the theme that death is a passage from this life to a new and everlasting life promised by Christ. It is a time of sadness for the loved ones over their loss, but it is also a time of joy for the deceased, who goes to eternal life. A person's good works or sins during their life on earth will by judged by God, resulting in a final resting place in either heaven or hell. Catholics believe there is a purgatory (limbo) in which souls can still be redeemed. The body or ashes must be buried, and a wake or viewing may precede the funeral mass. The community and the church support mourners through the wake and funeral service.

Hinduism. Death is a part of the continuing cycle of birth, life, death, and rebirth; the soul of the body transfers to another body after death. Prior to cremation, the body is bathed, laid in a coffin, and wrapped in white cloth. During the cremation ceremony, the body is carried counterclockwise, making three circles before it is placed on the pyre. The days of mourning are a time of ritual impurity, and the length of the mourning period varies. The Hindu culture values each part of the life cycle; elders are respected for their wisdom and not viewed as a burden at the end of their lives.

Islam. There is another world after death for which Muslims should prepare during their lives on earth. Mourning rituals include prayers for the forgiveness of the deceased followed by a final *Janazah* prayer. The funeral practices involve bathing the corpse and wrapping it in a *kafan,* or a plain cloth. Cremation is forbidden according to Islamic law, and only burial in the ground is allowed.

Judaism. Life will eventually lead to resurrection in a world to come. The body is washed for purification, dressed in a plain linen shroud and is buried as soon as possible. The body is watched over from the time of death until burial as a sign of respect; the kaddish, a prayer in honor of the dead, is said. Family members cease all worldly activities for seven days from the time of death; this is known as *sitting shiva*. The full mourning period lasts a year until the dead person's *yahrzeit*, or yearly anniversary of death.

Do Different Cultures Prepare Final Good-byes?

The review of religious death beliefs and rituals offers contextual perspectives. But it does not provide documentation of culturally sanctioned final good-byes as a form of death preparation. So my next research task focused on this. I located research on death preparation practices of Asian American and Hispanic cultures, fast-growing ethnic minorities in the United States. I also interviewed a very small sample of people from several different countries and cultures. I decided to conduct interviews because I suspected that if I could not find the information I was searching for in journals or electronic databases, it might be posited within individual people or families.

Asian American Cultures. Kathryn Braun and Rhea Nichols conducted a descriptive study of death and dying beliefs in four Asian American cultures: Chinese, Japanese, Vietnamese, and Filipino. [24] Chinese Americans have three traditional philosophies: *Confucianism,* an ethical system that emphasizes specific rituals throughout life and the belief that one's spirit lives beyond physical death; *Taoism,* which emphasizes longevity and reincarnation; and *Buddhism* (described in the previous section). Braun and Nichols reported that the completion of advance directives is becoming more acceptable among Chinese Americans. People in this study who were Buddhist reported that they are generally encouraged to talk about and plan for death, and many temple members have living wills. Few Vietnamese Americans were familiar with the concept of advance directives. Filipino Americans who had become associated with social service agencies were more comfortable with advance directives, while others were not comfortable planning for death.

Results from this study illustrate how death preparation and practices are affected by social norms that are rooted in religious beliefs. Results also show that death beliefs and practices are affected by cultural changes. There was no report of a custom similar to preparing Final Words in this study.

Mexican and Hispanic Cultures. To the indigenous people of Mexico, death is considered the passage to a new life. According to Ricardo Salvador, Mexican people have celebrated *Dia de Los Muertos,* or Day of the Dead, since ancient times.[25] Spanning two days (November 1 and 2), it is described as a beautiful ritual in which people happily and lovingly remember relatives who have died. Specific rituals vary from region to region, but traditionally one could expect to see whole towns decorated with flowers, squares filled with stands that offer colorful figures allusive to death, and festivals to honor *angelitos* ("little angels," or children) who have died. The essence of this celebration is to honor the lives of dead relatives, and in this way, give meaning and continuity to human existence. According to Salvador, such rituals now hold less religious and cultural importance in urban areas of Mexico.

Given this communal celebration of the dead, I wondered how it might influence death preparation rituals for Mexican and other Hispanic populations. Michael Kearl states that despite a surface appearance of death acceptance, this does not translate into a death-accepting culture in Mexico. [26] Beyond Mexico there is limited but growing research regarding the Latino culture's grieving process and death beliefs. According to Frances Munet-Vilaro, death is seen as an extension of life in some Latino cultures, and this belief seems to be beneficial in the grieving process.[27] Munet-Vilaro also reports that end-of-life care is discussed within the family context, rather than as an individual decision. I found no reported documentation of rituals to ensure personal good-byes in this review of Hispanic cultures.

Europe: Germany, Italy, United Kingdom. While visiting Tuscany, in east central Italy, I had the opportunity to meet with six middle-aged adults (four women and two men) who represented three different countries: Italy, the United Kingdom, and Germany. I described the idea of Final Words and inquired whether a custom of ensuring final personal messages exists in their countries. People from Germany and the United Kingdom stated with certainty that an oral or written custom like this did not exist in their countries. They speculated that if such a custom were practiced, it might be done on an individual or family basis. Italy, however, appears to have some type of final good-bye ritual. This interviewee reported that people sometimes write a letter to express final good-byes to community members. It is called an "epitaph" and is customarily printed in a newspaper. Italian epitaphs are not common and are primarily written by wealthy people. This epitaph differs from the one most people are familiar with—that is, an inscription on a tombstone or a summary statement about the deceased.

Excited about Italian epitaphs, I expected to easily find more information back in the United States. When general Internet searches led only to traditional epitaphs, I also searched genealogy Web sites and message boards. This led me to Salvatore Romano, an Italian genealogist from Trentino, a valley in northern Italy surrounded by mountains, castles, and lakes. With his exposure to numerous obituaries and family reports, I hoped he might know something about epitaphs. Romano reported he was unaware of these epitaphs or any formal custom for writing final personal messages.[28] But he did state that he had recently come across some final letters that parents had written to their children to express words of love. Romano emphasized that the letters were rare and did not reflect a cultural practice.

Nepal. A twenty-two-year-old female U.S. college student from a rural area near Katmandu, Nepal, was interviewed about death preparation practices. She reported that this culture has oral rituals involving end-of-life directives, and the main purpose is to determine property rights. Decisions about future living arrangements and property inheritance are conveyed early in life through this oral ritual. Thus, the son or daughter with whom an elder will spend the end of their life receives more property and material possessions. In case of a sudden death, the properties and possessions are normally and automatically transferred to the son. This Nepalese woman reported that it is not a customary practice to leave written (or oral) final personal messages to loved ones.

China. Information about death preparation rituals in China was provided by a thirty-nine-year-old woman born in Nanjing, China, who moved to the United States in her mid-twenties. She reported that Chinese people are very uncomfortable talking about death; doing so is almost ominous. Only when people are close to dying (very old or sick) would they begin to talk about their death and how the family members should share properties and take care of one another. She also reported that Chinese people do not use a legal last will and testament to bequeath material possessions. Rather it is expected that families will take care of one another, and this is communicated verbally between family members at the end of one's life. Thus, Chinese people do not have a formal ritual of writing final personal messages.

A New Cross-Cultural Social Norm

My research sought to discover the existence of rituals similar to Final Words or Legacy Letters. Toward this end, I reviewed research within the death and dying literature and examined death beliefs among major religions and several cultures. It is important to acknowledge the limitations of these efforts. Reviewing every possible source of information that might reveal the existence of culturally prescribed final messages is a daunting task and was not undertaken for this book. Information from broader cultures may not adequately reflect subcultures therein, thus limiting the ability to generalize beyond the described samples. Also, although I did not locate culturally prescribed rituals for final good-byes, this does not necessarily mean none exist. Perhaps as information about writing final messages spreads, it may spark discussions among people and help uncover whether such a ritual already exists within the many cultures not represented in this book. With the limitations of the scope of this research identified, results from my cross-cultural review of death beliefs, death rituals, and death preparation practices are summarized.

Ultimately, it seems that death preparation, in the form of personal and final good-byes, does not appear to exist as a widespread cultural practice in the United States or in the cultures I explored. The closest practice that exists on a widespread level involves advance directives for end-of-life medical or health care—in other words, the living will. The Italian custom of self-publishing an epitaph is the most similar ritual to Final Words, yet it does not appear to be widely practiced. Thus, it appears that the current venues for conveying personal good-byes appear to be the ethical will, hospice legacies, and personal letters. Yet none of these have risen to a level of tradition in mainstream culture. Although there is an organized response to the necessary details of death, there does not appear to be an organized ritual for the *emotional* preparation of final good-byes.

Another theme revealed in this research is how people talk—or don't talk—about death. It is clear that culturally unique rituals and mourning practices are created to facilitate completion of universal tasks of grief resolution and support the healing process. Cultures that may be more comfortable planning ahead for end-of-life care (e.g., Chinese Americans and Nepalese) appear freer to talk about details surrounding their death. Yet these details focus on end-of-life care; they do not ritualize the expression of a final, personal good-bye. As suggested previously, one emerging cultural trend in the United States that may provide an opening for the development of final messages on a larger scale includes advance directives found in the living will.

A last theme that can be identified involves how worldwide cultural rituals change. Death and dying rituals appear to be continually influenced by historical, social, economic, and traumatic events. They are also influenced simply by need; the physical and material aspects of death preparation and death are real and must be attended to. It would be good if we could broaden our definition of *need* to include the emotional as well as the physical. Gaining cross-cultural perspectives about death rituals and practices serves to increase the conversations we have about death preparation in our own cultures. And maybe new ideas like creating healing legacies will someday be absorbed into death education and death preparation rituals.

It will always be less painful to focus on the details of bequeathing material possessions than the emotional experience of saying good-bye. Not wanting to face that final parting is a universal experience. So is grief. But expressing personal final messages through Final Words and Legacy Letters can heal some of this grief. And perhaps it can also become a new social norm across cultures.

꩜ CHAPTER **4** ꩜

WRITING FINAL WORDS

THINKING ABOUT WHAT to say in a final message to the most significant people in your life can be overwhelming in many ways. When I first sat down to write Final Words to my husband and daughters, I was surprised by how difficult it was to begin. I had never faced this inevitable reality quite so honestly. I felt weighed down by an odd juxtaposition of two realities: I didn't ever want my death to happen, and yet at the same time, I knew that someday it would. Then things changed in a wonderful way.

Although the odd combination of death denial and death certainty made me feel sad (sadder than I could have imagined), once I began writing, I became aware of something that extended beyond the sadness. Or perhaps it grew out of this emotion. I can best describe it as sense of mission. I realized that I would be giving something to my family that only I could give: a healing legacy. And since I was writing to them when I was not at the end of my life, many possibilities still lay ahead, many opportunities to get things right.

What to Expect

Your experience may differ from mine. You may not see this bigger picture. You may not feel sad at all. Or you may cry so hard you cannot write. People have different worldviews as well as different temperaments. People can also differ in the ability to feel. Cultural rules often teach us to ignore our feelings, especially the more painful or vulnerable ones. After a while it is possible to blunt—or not even feel—emotions. Boys and men know these lessons better than anyone else (as discussed in chapter 7). Regardless of the differences we may bring to the experience of writing Final Words, we can all imagine just how important such words might be.

Once you start writing, a range of issues will rise to the surface. Some are predictable and some will be unexpected. Some are easy and some will be difficult. But one common thread binds all the issues together: everything takes on a different meaning in light of the perspective from which you are writing. As mentioned previously, I refer to this as the eternity perspective. A personal example of this involves my husband and me. The first time I wrote Final Words to him, we were in the midst of round twenty-two of a conflict that had waxed and waned throughout our marriage. Writing a final message to him did not instantly make everything better. But I can honestly say that something shifted inside as I viewed our con-flict from the eternity perspective—what our lives would be like without the other one in it. More specifically, I had a new-found motivation to resolve that conflict. This motivation probably wasn't too different from what occurs when people have a near-death experience or recover from a terminal ill-ness. Also mentioned previously, this renewed sense to improve life can be a positive result from writing Final Words.

It may be difficult to imagine any positive experiences before you begin writing. They may not come to you right away; and they may not come at all. That's all right. But I do think you will experience the benefits of seeing things in a new and truthful light. It actually took several months until my husband and I finally resolved that conflict. But the motiva-tion started when I began writing Final Words. I hope you have a similar experience.

It is relatively easy to think about writing Final Words to someone with whom you have a wonderful relationship. I hope my personal example suggests that it's also possible to write Final Words to someone with whom you are in conflict. In addition to shadow work, various resources exist to help you work through resistance or conflict when writing to loved ones. It is well worth the effort for many reasons, the least of which is how it can improve your current relationships.

Who to Write

When considering the significant people in your life to whom you may be writing final messages, it is obvious that if you have a partner or spouse and children, you will write to them.

And if your parents, siblings, and grandparents are alive, you will also likely write to them. What can happen at this point is that you start thinking of so many people—aunts and uncles, cousins, nieces and nephews, friends, colleagues, mechanics, doctors, and so forth—that the next thing you know, you're afraid you will need to take vacation time to get letters written to all of them.

Not to worry. I found myself starting to think this way as I reflected upon all the people I love and to whom I want to give final messages. But the more I thought about it, the more I realized there were fewer than ten people in my life who *really need* a healing legacy from me. Writing nine different letters was not overwhelming. And since I enjoy writing, it was a positive and meaningful experience, almost like a mini retreat. But if you do not like to write, or if you find writing many different letters to be overwhelming, there are alternatives. You can write a group letter. You could also do a combination, perhaps writing an individual letter to your spouse or partner and a group letter to everyone else. The issue of group versus individual Final Words is addressed more fully later in this chapter, but I mention group letters here to allay any concerns that may be arising as you begin to think about all the different people in your life. Also to let you know that if there are others in your life who would benefit from a final message but who don't need an individual legacy, a group letter would be appropriate. This might include groups such as colleagues, neighbors, board members, church or temple worshippers, a team, or an institution. Described in this way, such a letter would be similar to the Italian epitaph.

Use the following process as a guide to help you identify the people who may benefit from receiving a healing legacy from you:

- Close your eyes and ask yourself, *Who needs a healing legacy from me?*
- Wait.
- Pay attention to who comes to mind.
- Open your eyes and write their names.
- Start here.

Take as long as you need to identify these people. You may want to go through these steps several times, perhaps on different days or months. If other people came to mind who don't need a healing legacy from you, but for whom you wish to leave a final message of some type, create another list of that nature. Revise both lists as needed.

Ready, Set, Write

After deciding to write Final Words, the main challenge for most of us is finding the time to do the thinking and the writing. The following section is intended to help with this process. And though *ready, set, write* is a catchy little phrase, it is actually very accurate. You must be ready before you write. Much of the readiness happens by reading this book, reflecting on the meaning and process of writing Final Words, and then making a commitment to write. Getting set refers to setting aside the time and space. And writing is the tool you will use to create a healing legacy. Below are more specific suggestions for beginning.

Getting Started

Forgive the echo of the 1980s slogan *Just Say No,* but the solution to getting started is as straightforward—*Just Start.* There will always be dozens of daily details that compete for your time and attention. And they may be more important in the immediate sense of things. But creating a healing legacy is more important in the forever sense. I don't have to explain this point further—you know what I mean.

We all have different ways of starting momentous projects. When my husband and I were first married, he decided to start his doctoral dissertation by announcing the day and time he planned to begin: he would start writing his dissertation the following Saturday morning. This intelligent and successful person, who rarely thinks about cleaning, decided not only to clean our coffeemaker but also to rewire it so the "on" light would work again on that very same Saturday morning. As morning turned into afternoon and he was still at work renovating the coffeemaker, I tentatively suggested that he might be procrastinating about working on his dissertation. He was indignant at my suggestion. Rather, he insisted he was indulging in a small, frivolous task before undertaking an epic one.

I share this endearing story to illustrate two points. First, many things can get in the way of starting something important. They may be big or small, fun or toil, important or mundane (like coffeemakers). Second, sometimes the roadblocks are out of our awareness; we really don't know why we can't get started. So if you're the type of person who needs help getting started or following through, here are some strategies. For the type of person who needs structure, try beginning with something as simple as adding "Final Words" to your weekend to-do list. If this seems too easy to ignore, give yourself a deadline and mark it on your calendar. It may also help to treat Final Words with the same urgency with which you approach completing your last will and testament. Plan ahead for the specific date and time, the way you would schedule any appointment. Put it in your calendar or your handheld computer. Then simply keep the appointment with yourself.

There are some naturally motivating times that can also prompt you to write Final Words. This includes when you are preparing to travel without your family or loved ones, or if you plan to be involved in an experience that involves higher than normal risk for harm—for example, sky diving, scuba diving, or hang gliding. Downhill skiing and plane travel could be included here, too. (And in many areas, simply driving the interstate may also qualify.) The main idea here is that as you anticipate situations that have higher potential for mortality, you will likely feel more compelled to begin writing. So look for these occasions to motivate you.

For those who need more accountability or external motivation than the previous suggestions, another strategy is to create community around the process by involving others. Not unlike those who prefer to exercise with a buddy, or those who need external support to stay on a diet, go ahead and ask a person to be an accountability coach for writing Final Words. You might ask your partner, a parent, or a friend. But do remember that after you request their assistance, they have the right to nag you and say, "Have you written your Final Words yet?" Rather than grumble about being nagged, you would then respond, "Thanks for the reminder—I'll do it today." Another helpful way to begin writing is to meditate or pray. Each of us has different ways to transcend ourselves. Some people use formal practices of meditation and prayer, some create their own means. As for me, before I began to write Final Words, I asked God to guide me and to keep my heart open to grace.

After people write their first Final Words to someone, it becomes much easier to write the second, third, fourth, and so on. Other people have described this similar pattern to me. There is just something about the first one that seems to create the most anxiety or anticipation. So without belaboring the point further, I'll conclude by restating that the best way to get started is simply to . . . *just start.*

What to Say

Deciding what to say is a very personal matter. You may know exactly what to say ahead of time, or you may figure it out as you go along. Since the intention of Final Words is to provide loved ones with a healing legacy, your message may have the effect of expressing love, asking for or granting forgiveness, mending a relationship, offering hope, passing on family values, healing a wound, providing words of wisdom, offering a blueprint for getting through life, helping others learn from your mistakes, providing spiritual direction, or professing a much needed expression of love. Your message will also provide a necessary good-bye. But when all the effects of Final Words are combined, what you are really doing is honoring the relationship you have with these loved ones.

Another factor that can help you determine what to say involves considering how and when your words will be read. If they will be read privately and individually, this will guide your writing. If your Final Words will be read out loud to a group of your loved ones, this will also guide you. And if others will be listening who are not directly addressed, this too will guide what you say. For example, if you decide ahead of time that you want your final messages to be read at a funeral service, the words you write for a public venue will likely differ from those you write for a more private reading. Deciding ahead of time on the likely setting in which your final messages will be read can help create a backdrop for your story to unfold.

Since all of us benefit when someone else's suggestion sparks an idea of our own, I have provided an outline that may also help guide your writing final messages to a loved one. (Please skip past this section if you would rather craft a narrative that is entirely unique.) Sample formats with detailed sentence starters for individual and group Final Words are also provided in the appendix section. You can use the following outline as is, adapt it, or ignore it. At the very least, I sincerely hope it generates ideas for you:

- Briefly describe the present time (today's date, your age and health, and if you wish, the age and health of the person to whom you are writing).
- State your purpose for writing.
- Describe what is wonderful about this person.
- Review what you value about your relationship with this person.

- Recall any meaningful moments or memories.
- Communicate any spiritual or religious messages.
- If aspects of the relationship were not always positive, healthy, or helpful, acknowledge this. If you were responsible for all or part of it, offer a sincere apology; if you were hurt or victimized by this person, and if you truly forgive him or her, say so.
- Express your values, wishes, hopes, dreams, life lessons, spiritual or religious beliefs. Write as much or as little as you wish.
- If you hope this person will take special care of someone with special needs (elderly parent, spouse, young child, etc.), state your wishes. Don't request the impossible; be reasonable in your expectations.
- In preparing to close, say how you would like the person to remember you.
- Express gratitude and thanks.
- Express your love.
- Say farewell and sign your name.

Remember that the reader will cherish every word, regardless of how plain or eloquent you write. It is the heart behind your message that creates the healing legacy.

Where to Write

A workshop can be a wonderful venue to write Final Words for several reasons. Workshops force you to set aside time for writing. They create a caring and serious atmosphere. They also provide a facilitator who can provide "technical consultation" as well as personal support. Other workshop attendees can be a resource for processing and sharing. You may soon be able to locate a writing workshop in your area at community centers and houses of worship. Internet-based workshops are another possible venue. It is my sincere hope that as interest increases in writing Final Words, trained facilitators will be available to meet the demand.

Many people, especially introverts, may prefer to work at their own pace in the privacy of their own home. And this is fine, too. The place doesn't matter as much as simply starting—and finishing—the process. I have written Final Words while traveling up the interstate (as a passenger, of course) with my family in the car. I have written Final Words in my office on a lunch hour. I have also written Final Words while sitting on the meditation bench beside our creek. Wherever you choose to write, be sure to find a place, wherever it may be, where you will be free of distractions.

If there isn't a writing workshop nearby, or if you prefer to work in your own space and at your own pace, then the best time to write Final Words is now. And the best place is wherever you can create a quiet and focused space.

What Is the Best Length?

You probably know the answer to this before I make a suggestion: there is no absolute length. This means that the best length could be short or long. And both would be "right." Most of my Final Words have been about a page, single-spaced. For parents who wish to address many significant milestones that lay ahead for their children, the final messages will be longer (chapter 8 includes many more suggestions for parents). Overall, the best way to measure how long your Final Words should be is to simply write down what you want to say to this person or group of people. Then read it over and ask yourself if there is anything left unsaid. If so, add on. If not, you have the best length.

Verb Tense

When you write your Final Words, you may become confused about which verb tense to use. I know I was. The confusion involves the fact that you are writing while you're alive, but you know it will be read when you are not (unless you plan to give it earlier, which is always an option). The possible verb tenses include: Present tense, *I love you with all my heart;* Past or past perfect tense, *I loved you; I have loved you with all my heart,* or Future tense, *I will always love you.* The tense you choose is entirely up to you. But I do have a few recommendations. Write a few sentences and see which verb tense makes the most sense. Read the Final Words of someone else (at a workshop or the samples in this book) and see what sounds best. Another suggestion is to think about verb tenses you use in letter writing. Letters often begin with present tense and change to fit the content and pacing of the message. A linear example follows:

- Start in the present: *I am writing these words to you when I am forty-five years old and in good health. You are forty and also in good health.*
- Move to past or past perfect: *I loved being your wife;*

> *I have treasured the role of being your husband over the years . . .*

- End with future tense: *I will always love you*; or *I hope you will take good care of Dad*; or *I hope you find a purpose in life that makes you happy to get up everyday.*

You can see how these verb tenses shift and mirror the narrative flow of an everyday letter that you might write to someone. This familiar flow can be very comforting for the reader. All these suggestions notwithstanding, I encourage you to write in the verb tense(s) that best reflects your message.

Finding the Right Voice

The tone with which you write will vary depending on to whom you are writing. These variations can include the age of the person (child or adult) as well as the relationship (son or father). Adjusting your writing style will come naturally in the same way you adjust when talking with people of different ages. In other words, you don't talk to a six-year-old the way you talk with a sixty-year-old. Most of my Final Words were written in a tender and hopeful tone. So I was surprised when I found myself almost being "chatty" while writing Final Words to a relative. I had to stop and ask myself, *Is this how I want my last message to be for this person?* As it turns out, the answer was yes, because that tone reflected our relationship. So please trust that you will write in a way that fits the relationship and reflects the unique characteristics of the person.

There is something else that is important about the voice of your Final Words. You may notice while writing that there is another "voice" that guides this whole process, and it tends to speak in a similar way to everyone. It is difficult to describe, but I think you will recognize it when you begin writing your final messages. What is even more interesting is that this same voice can be heard in the Final Words of *others* as well. Maybe it's wisdom. Maybe it's love. Or maybe it's the sound of healing.

So speak from your heart and don't worry about the specifics. Just begin writing and let the healing voice come to you.

More Essentials

People often have many questions before they start to write their Final Words. And as they begin writing, additional questions emerge. All of this is to be expected. Here are some common questions and issues.

Handwritten or Typewritten? What about Audio- or Videotaping?

Since my handwriting is terrible, I used a computer to write and print my Final Words and then signed them. I believe handwritten Final Words are better than computer-generated or typewritten pages, because handwriting is more personal. But the best way to decide on this issue may be to craft a narrative with which you are most comfortable and most likely to finish.

There are pros and cons to any method of writing Final Words. Computer-printed narratives are impersonal, but much easier to revise or totally rewrite. The final messages I wrote to my children have been easy to update over the years, since I have saved them electronically. Most children today are accustomed to reading e-mails, instant messaging, and using other modern types of communication. They are less familiar with the handwritten letter or note as a way of communicating. To them, computer-printed final messages may be personal enough. This may also be true for adults who are accustomed to technology, too. But let me go on record here as saying that I don't think anything can ever replace a handwritten letter.

For many people, some form of electronic or digital media may be a more practical or comfortable way to express Final Words. These narratives can be created and stored on audio/videotape, CD, or DVD. Though expressing Final Words in one of these forms may be the way to go for a variety of reasons, I advocate putting the actual words in printed form so that your loved ones can hold them in their hands, where they are tangible and concrete. If a disability or illness prevents you from writing or typing, your words can be dictated to a trusted person who can then transcribe them for you.

Having stated my fondness and respect for the written word, final messages can of course be created and saved in any medium, for whatever reason. If you don't have a preference, another option is to ask your loved ones if they have a preference.

Individual versus Group Final Words?

I like writing individual Final Words to individual people. This is partly because I see and experience relationships as being unique. However, many people may see and experience their relationships as being less individualized or unique. If this is the case, they may prefer to write final messages to groups rather than to individuals. The sample ethical will presented in chapter 1 was written to a man's family and was signed by "Dad and Grandpa." All that needed to be said was expressed in this way. Those who receive a group letter may prefer an individual letter, but a healing legacy can be provided either way. A beautiful example of final messages written to a group by a man named Billy Flowers can be found in chapter 9.

A last comment about group versus individual Final Words: it is important to let your loved ones emerge as individuals in some way, because the essence of Final Words is about honoring relationships. Perhaps the best way to decide about whether to write group or individual final messages is just to begin writing and trust that the best format will create itself.

Getting Feedback

The first place to start getting feedback is from yourself. Our fast-paced culture doesn't foster much (if any) inward reflection, but self-reflection is an important aspect of most life experiences and social interactions. One way to give feedback to yourself about your Final Words is simply to read them, silently or out loud. Pause and let the weight and meaning of your words take root. Notice how you feel. Pay attention to any random thoughts or reactions. Make notes in the margins. Or if your words seem to be complete, enjoy the satisfaction of having written them. If not, keep going. They are often a work in progress.

Another way to create feedback for yourself is to imagine

your Final Words being read by the person or group you are addressing. Imagine the setting. Take on their grief. Then ask yourself how you want the person(s) to think or feel after reading your message. Now make changes as you see fit.

If you decide that you want feedback from others, the likely places to look are people you trust: a spouse, partner, religious person, spiritual director, or just a tried-and-true friend. When asking someone to read your Final Words, be specific about the kind of feedback you need. You may ask the reader to check and see if you conveyed a specific message clearly enough. You may ask for feedback about the overall tone of voice. Or you may ask what might be "missing" from an objective point of view.

Keep in mind that another valuable part of the feedback process is to step away from your writing for a bit. This might mean taking a walk during or after your writing. The break might be a few minutes or it may be a week. Leaving time between start and finish can allow new ideas and messages to emerge. Your break could include talking with someone about your process. It could also involve meditation, contemplation, or prayer. If you are writing your Final Words while attending a workshop, fellow participants will be another excellent source of objective feedback.

Getting feedback about anything is helpful. But I tend to think that the writer knows best what to say and how to say it. So get feedback if you need reassurance, but remember, *you* are the real expert about what your loved ones need to hear from you.

Revising

If you get feedback that makes you want to change your Final Words, then revisions will naturally follow. It is entirely possible that Final Words can be written in such a way that we don't need to revise them much. While we may always think of something else to tell a loved one, core messages are usually timeless and complete. You have said all you need to say.

But this is not always the case. There are times when you will want—and need—to revise your final messages. One example includes writing to young children. Since their needs change over time, this may prompt a desire to change your tone of voice or words to match their new developmental stage (writing to children is discussed in detail in chapter 8.) Another time when final messages might need to be revised is when a relationship shifts. If the quality of a relationship has changed from good to bad, or bad to good, you will want this to be reflected in your healing legacy to that person. I know someone that has kept their original Final Words exactly the same. But every so often, she adds a handwritten postscript. The update is often just a line or two. The absence of her need to keep rewriting Final Words is a testament to the timelessness and wholeness with which Final Words are usually written.

Keep in mind that it is entirely possible to revise your Final Words as often or as much as you'd like. Thanks to the technology of computers, digital recording, and good old reliable paper and pen, we can change them with ease whenever we want. Despite the timeless nature of Final Words, I do think it's a good idea to review them occasionally and to make revisions accordingly. If you forget to revise your final messages, don't worry. Just be sure to write them once and trust in your heartfelt expressions.

Where to Keep Final Words?

I suggest keeping your Final Words with your last will and testament. This may be located with a trusted attorney, friend, or family member. You may also decide to keep a copy with other important documents in your home or office. I know someone who keeps a copy in a desk drawer in her office (in the same folder with a copy of her last will and testament). To set the Final Words apart from the legal document, she has placed each final message in an envelope with the person's name handwritten on the front. Her signature is written over the seal. I put all of my Final Words together in one envelope and keep it with my last will and testament. I have copies in separate geographic locations. This way, if something happened at one place, my Final Words would still exist in the other.

To guarantee that Final Words will remain safe from a variety of potential natural and manmade disasters, consider making several duplicates. These could be stored in different geographic locations, perhaps sending a copy for safekeeping to a trusted friend or family member in a different state. You could also make electronic versions saved to disc, CD, or an Internet Web site or other cyber venue.

If you decide not to keep your Final Words with your last will and testament, you can make sure the location of your Final Words is known by including a note with your will that describes the location. You could also write the location of your Final Words on a small card that is kept in your wallet with a driver's license. This would be a fitting place, since many driver's licenses include our donor information, another life legacy. If you have a living will, keeping your Final Words with that document is another good place.

In keeping with the flexible tone of previous suggestions, please keep your healing legacies wherever you wish. Just be aware of the need to protect them and that the most important criterion (after writing them) is to tell someone their location.

Reading Final Words

Final Words are intended to be read after your death. You may also elect to have them read at another time while you are alive, as has recently occurred with ethical wills. While the desire to leave nothing unsaid when you are still alive is important and should be honored, I suggest that this be done through a different type of communication and let the Final Words be read after your death. The next chapter describes Legacy Letters as an alternative communication to be read while you are still alive. Mentioned previously, there are two types of Legacy Letters. One is written to a loved one who will likely die before you; the other is written to express celebration, gratitude, or reconciliation and is not associated with the end of life.

I also mention Legacy Letters here if you are not ready to write Final Words or if you prefer to try to leave nothing left unsaid now, rather than after your death. Some of us may be limited by death denial and fear, while others may desire relationship transformation *now* through a healing letter. Discussed further in the next chapter, there is certainly enough time during the course of our lives to write all three narratives (Final Words and both types of Legacy Letters).

Years before I thought about these ideas, I wrote a letter of gratitude to my mother during the first year I was a mother. I wanted to acknowledge all the selfless caregiving work she had provided to our family over the years. Until that time, I hadn't really understood my mom's lifelong sacrifices and how unappreciated they were. I needed to walk in her daily footsteps as a mother myself, becoming foggy with exhaustion, endless details, and laundry. I also had to go day after day without adult companionship—or a paycheck—to really "get it." During that first year as a tired new mom (with only one child), I couldn't fathom how my mother had done this three times. I wrote the letter as a celebration of her life at the time. She still has that letter.

Overcoming Ordinary Resistance

You may decide that writing Final Words is important. And you may decide that you want to write them. But sometimes opposition gets the upper hand and prevents you from doing what you want or need to do. Opposition to writing Final Words can come in many forms. Chapter 2 focused on inner forms of resistance such as shadow, unresolved grief, and personality traits and temperament. Death denial and fear were also recognized as other types of resistance. But there are also the more ordinary struggles that get in the way, such as: *I don't have time; I just don't want to; I have nothing to say; It's too*

painful. While all of these may be true, and indeed a natural response to something very difficult, they only become a problem if they prevent you from writing your Final Words.

If you experience this ordinary resistance to writing final messages, I recommend a "homeopathic remedy." The basic philosophy of homeopathy is "treating like with like." Rather than fight the symptom or problem, use it. Go with it. Applying this remedy to ordinary resistance, the first step is simply to name the problem. Admit to yourself that you are resisting writing Final Words by filling in the blank: *I'm not writing final messages because . . . I don't have time; I don't know what to say;* or whatever your reason is. The next thing to do is to agree with yourself: *That's right, I am way too busy to do this; I really don't want to write these Final Words . . . who would?* or *I have no idea how to begin or what to say.* What follows next is simple. Once you've identified and accepted the difficulty, you can then tell yourself that you don't have to write Final Words. This is important, because it is true. You don't *have* to write them to anyone.

You probably see the beauty of this by now. Going with the resistance means you no longer have to fight the opposition. With this interference removed, you're left with the obvious: if you don't want to write Final Words, you don't have to—and if you don't, no one else will.

WRITING LEGACY LETTERS

WE GIVE AND receive legacies. They come to us as gifts, symbols, bequests, heritages, birthrights, and words. We also give and receive healing. This, too, comes in different forms. A specific letter that combines healing and heritage is called a *Legacy Letter* of affirmation and good-bye given to a loved one at the end of his or her life. This letter can acknowledge a loved one's life achievement, express gratitude to them, recall memories, honor relationships, ask and grant forgiveness, or convey any other message that needs to be given, and received. Writing a Legacy Letter to a loved one who is likely to die before us complements the ritual of Final Words. Taken together, both ensure that nothing is left unsaid.

It is important to acknowledge that letters of affirmation

can be given to loved ones at any time—to celebrate a special birthday or life milestone, to apologize or ask forgiveness, or simply to express love and gratitude. We do not need to wait until the end of someone's life to write such an important letter. And indeed we don't. Writing letters to celebrate certain milestones and relationships is very common and as old as time immortal. I consider this form of writing to be another type of letter, which I refer to as a Legacy Letter of celebration, reconciliation, or gratitude.

I debated about whether to discuss both types of Legacy Letters in this book. Part of my reluctance involved how the letter of celebration might be viewed as an alternative to writing Final Words. To be sure, writing a letter that celebrates someone is much easier than thinking about his or her death. Then I took a step back and realized that this wasn't a problem at all. Any affirmation written to a loved one during their life contributes to healing. So while Final Words create the possibility for healing a loved one's grief, letters of celebration written throughout their lives are no less important. And those letters may even end up becoming a treasured final message or healing legacy from a loved one after they are gone, as was the case for me.

Mentioned in the previous chapter, perhaps the best way to approach the idea of important letters is to apply the rule of threes: (1) we can write Final Words to be read after our death, (2) we can write Legacy Letters of celebration or gratitude to loved ones at specific points in life, (3) and we can write Legacy Letters of affirmation and good-bye to those who may die before us. By doing all three, nothing is likely to go unsaid.

I realize that all of this may seem like "too much"—to do, to read, to keep track of. But when you compare the countless papers you have written for school or work to the amount of time involved with writing Final Words and Legacy Letters, writing healing legacies is clearly less than all of this "required" writing combined. Indeed, when my suggested trio of writings is spread across a person's lifespan, there is more than enough time to create written legacies like this for the people we care about most.

Expressing important messages to loved ones can extend beyond the boundaries of family to include friends and sometimes colleagues. No matter which type of letter is written, and no matter who the recipient is, writing Final Words and Legacy Letters can be a valuable exercise in emotional expression.

Writing as Emotional Expression: Research Findings

From my vantage point as a counselor and developmental psychologist, emotion and cognition are equally important. Psychologists who study the relationship between cognition and emotion suggest it is not possible to think a thought without having a simultaneous emotion. It also appears that emotions can directly affect our thinking ability.[1,2,3] To test the idea that emotions and thoughts are intertwined, say the following words and phrases to yourself, pausing a few seconds between them: *rain . . . dying . . . beach . . . vacation . . . high school reunion . . . turning fifty*. Though not a scientific experiment, you probably became aware that these words not only differ from one another in meaning, but they also convey something different within you. And I would suggest that this difference involves emotion.

Over the past decade, there has been increased interest and research in the area of emotional intelligence (EI), which has been defined differently by various researchers and writers, including Daniel Goleman, who published a book that brought popular attention to the subject.[4] I prefer to use the following four-pronged model when discussing emotional intelligence: (1) perceiving and expressing emotions, (2) integrating emotions with thoughts, (3) analyzing emotions, and (4) regulating emotions.[5] Each of the four EI skill sets merits in-depth discussion. For our purposes, the first category is our primary focus; perceiving and expressing emotions is a central skill for writing final personal messages.

Both Final Words and Legacy Letters involve emotional expression. Whether it is an end-of-life affirmation letter or a celebration of a life milestone along the way, our words express our feelings. The emotional aspect of writing can be affected by many factors, including personality, writing ability, and whether we have been socialized to express emotion. These three factors are addressed elsewhere in this book. Here I want to focus on what researchers are learning about the positive benefits of emotional expression.

The Power of the Written Word

Writing can be a tool that opens our minds and hearts to thoughts and emotions that are deep inside us. But that's not all. Writing can offer benefits that extend beyond emotional health.[6,7] The simple act of writing about bad times can be a potent and low-cost way to improve physical and emotional health, reports psychologist James Pennebaker, who has conducted decades of research into the healing effects of writing. His findings validate what many people have found incidentally through journal writing. When we create a cohesive personal narrative of our lives and link specific emotions to specific events, we have more knowledge and control of how those emotions and events affect our current lives.[8] Pennebaker suggests that although many of us might want to simply eliminate the pain in our lives, those who learn how to use that pain in a constructive way are often far healthier than those who do not. Indeed, studies have shown that participating in a writing process that expresses emotions can decrease a research participant's blood pressure, as well as the number of doctor office visits.[9] Additional research suggests that emotionally expressive writing can also reduce asthma symptoms and arthritis pain.[10]

Scientists do not fully understand why writing helps, but it appears that writing may bolster the immune function in some way.[11] Another psychological explanation is that writing helps us "work through" our issues. If everything that happens to us is somehow part of who we are, then writing may help us find order in these experiences—perhaps even as a form of self-analysis or as a way to give form and sense to what has affected us. As James Pennebaker says, "We don't need to talk to others to tell our untold stories. Nonetheless, our untold thoughts and feelings should, in some way, be verbalized. Whether we talk into a tape recorder or write on a magic pad, translating our thoughts into language is psychologically and physically beneficial. When people write about major upheavals, they begin to organize and understand them."[12]

In Pennebaker's studies people simply start writing about a specific event, experience, or relationship that affected them without planning to have anyone else read it.[13] Participants are instructed to write freely without stopping for at least twenty minutes a day for three consecutive days. They are told not to edit or worry about spelling or how things might sound. Instead they should focus on both the event and the emotions associated with the event. In other words, people are simply instructed to write and see what comes out.

Since writing Final Words and Legacy Letters does not follow the protocol outlined in Pennebaker's studies, a direct comparison between the two methods cannot be made. But a particular counseling technique can serve as a link between emotional expression and writing final messages. This technique is referred to as "unfinished business," a concept that originated with Gestalt therapy. Completing unfinished business purportedly helps free people from unwanted past messages, feelings, thoughts, and behaviors. Like most therapies, it is designed to help people resolve impediments to their wholeness and promote healthy interpersonal relationships. Building on the neuropsychological fact that our nervous system may not tell the difference between a real experience and a vividly imagined experience, Gestalt techniques help people work through unresolved past issues *in the present*.

One of these techniques involves writing a letter to provide closure to unfinished business. The letter is not intended to be sent, but rather to free a trapped thought or belief that has become frozen in time. Most therapists would likely agree that the ability of people to tell their own story provides the opportunity to fully understand that story—perhaps for the first time[14] Indeed, it appears there is something about the writing process that "changes things." When I have invited clients to write about an upsetting experience during a counseling session, many people have said that they didn't know what they were going to write about. But once they got started writing, they couldn't stop.

Regardless of the form our writing takes—unfinished business technique, journal writing, Legacy Letters, or Final Words —it appears that writing has the power to heal us and to help us grow. Or as Karen Congliosi suggests, "It can help us understand who we are and where and why we have formed positive and negative attachments. Writing can then help us redirect our energy . . . and get in touch with what is often hidden from us—whether it is the reason behind our weight gain, a hard-to-understand addiction, a compulsion we fight daily, or a pain we wish would go away. Writing helps us to form connections with what is going on inside us and with others."[15]

It is important to note that although it may be difficult for people to revisit painful emotions, over time, any discomfort appears to be short lived, and for most people the benefits far outweigh the initial costs. Not all studies report these same positive results, though,[16] so it may be that emotional expression through writing is more helpful for certain experiences and symptoms than for others. Nevertheless, "the writing cure" generally appears to promote health and emotional well-being.[17]

Perhaps most central to the task at hand, Final Words and Legacy Letters can serve as a way to complete important unfinished business, such as unsaid resentments, regrets, or apologies, as well as to celebrate life, honor relationships, and promote healing or reconciliation. Or they can simply restate something that we wish to make certain a loved one knows. The truth is that most of us experience a mixture of positive and negative experiences in our past and current relationships. It would make sense that our letters and final messages would reflect both. And based on the research reviewed, such written emotional expression is likely to be good for us. It might even be transformative.

What Do Legacy Letters Say?

Until you actually sit down and write, it is difficult to fully comprehend how writing final affirmation messages can transform you or the reader. I reviewed some of the research on written emotional expression and described the theory behind Gestalt therapy to offer one explanation for how this transformation occurs. Since our nervous system doesn't have a sense of time, we can revisit the past or step into the future during the present. This is pretty amazing when you think about it. When writing important words and letters, a transformation can occur as our brains let us transcend time to remember, to hope, and to heal. Perhaps this is one of those divine coping skills that help humans restore wholeness.

Your reasons for sitting down and writing a Legacy Letter will guide what we say. Those reasons range as far and wide as the human condition: a father heading away on a trip, a daughter recognizing her mother's life sacrifices when she becomes a mother herself, a father expressing pride upon a son's graduation, a father and son seeking reconciliation through apology and forgiveness, an adult daughter affirming a mother just weeks before the mother dies, a soldier heading off to war, a parent just wanting to make sure that nothing is left unsaid in case of sudden death. Each letter may differ according to the situation, but all will offer affirmation for the receiver and can establish a healing connection between the writer and the receiver. Perhaps more than any other written communication, Legacy Letters written to and from someone going into harm's way will reflect the tension between life and death.

Still it may not be clear what you will write to your loved ones. It may not even be clear that you have anything at all to say—and that's okay. Most likely what will happen is that since the writing of Legacy Letters is guided by your desire to express a specific message to someone, you will know *exactly* what to say once you sit down. A letter of celebration or gratitude usually flows from the heart. And a final letter of affirmation and good-bye may express love, pride, recognition, gratitude, apology, forgiveness, regrets, hopes, life lessons, family values, and treasured memories. You may even be tempted to reveal a secret. Though if this is the case, I strongly suggest that you be present when the letter is read to allow time for discussing the revelation in a face-to-face conversation.

Similar to the process of writing Final Words, you will be faced with a decision about whether to write individual letters or whether to write a group letter. There are no external guidelines for this determination. The guidelines come from within you. If you want to mark a specific milestone in someone's life, an individual letter is obviously most appropriate. In fact,

Legacy Letters generally lend themselves to an individual format, though at times you may have reason or need to write a letter to a group of people or an organization.

Letters of Celebration and Gratitude

As I began discussing Final Words and Legacy Letters of good-bye with people, I learned that neither is a widely practiced ritual. But many people told me they had written some type of letter to a loved one to express an intimate message or to recognize a special occasion or milestone. This typically involved a significant birthday for a son or daughter (e.g., eighteenth) or an aging parent (e.g., sixty-fifth). Another example included recognizing celebratory events, such as a wedding anniversary, or a rite of passage, such as high school or college graduation. I also learned that adult children can be prompted to write a letter to their parents after recovering from adolescent rebellion or to express gratitude to parents. I wrote letters of gratitude to both of my parents at different points in life. And I'm really glad I did.

The tone of such letters reflects gratitude, joy, and pride. It may also convey regret about a past hurt or for granting forgiveness, resulting in reconciliation. Letters like this have some common ground with Final Words. One shared feature is that the purpose of both is essentially to express intimate thoughts and feelings, to affirm another person, and to *honor the relationship* between the writer and receiver. Also like Final Words, the writer of a Legacy Letter often intends to leave nothing unsaid at the time the letter is written. Although many of these letters are exchanged between parents and children, such letters can be

(and are) written between anyone. Friends and romantic partners may be moved at different points to create a permanent testimony to the relationship. People typically experience much
less resistance to writing Legacy Letters as compared to writing
Final Words, probably due to the absence of finality or death.

As I continued to talk about the idea of Final Words and
Legacy Letters with different people, I learned more from
those who write them. As they described letters of affirmation,
love, and celebration, they seemed happy and peaceful. Some
of the letters were written to sons and daughters, others to
mothers and fathers. A few of these letters have been shared
throughout this book. As described to me, the letters were
carefully written and intended to be a legacy. Some were
purely for celebration, while others were intended to heal relationships or soul scars.

Unlike the ritual of Final Words, which lends itself to a
structured format or review of life, Legacy Letters of celebration will vary according to the situation or milestone that
prompts your desire to write. So I have not provided a specific
format for this letter. Instead, I share stories about people who
have written these letters with the hope they will inspire you
to write your own. Chapter 8 includes parents letters to
teenagers. The following story is about a letter written by an
adult daughter to her father.

Ruth's Legacy Letter

When I described the idea of Final Words to Ruth, a woman
in her late thirties, she listened politely and declared that this
ritual wasn't needed. She believed that we say everything we

need to say when we are alive. She then went on to tell why she believes this. Ruth and her father had been estranged until her early twenties. She wistfully reminisced how, after recovering from a rebellious period in her life, she had written her father a letter. In the letter, Ruth told her father how much she loved him and apologized for any hurt she had caused him by her behaviors. She expressed regret about having cut off communication with him during her rebellious years. He never responded to that letter.

Ruth paused during this part of the story, but there wasn't a trace of sadness or resentment in her voice. Her face was radiating. Since this didn't match what she had just shared, I was puzzled. And though I was bursting to say more about my idea and try to convince her of its merit, I sensed there was more to this story and that I had something to learn. And this was certainly the case. Though Ruth's father never acknowledged the letter, their relationship gradually improved after she gave it to him. They became emotionally closer as both began to directly express affection and concern to each other amid life's daily happenings. They were also able to share time together at the end of his life and exchange meaningful final good-byes. Though Ruth sensed that the letter she had written to her father years ago helped improve their relationship, she never knew for sure, because he never said anything about it. As it turns out, during the intimately heavy burden of going through her father's belongings after his death, she found the letter she had written to him many years ago. It was folded up in his billfold. Like their relationship, the paper had become softer over time. And he had carried it with him every day.

A true story like this brings hope for mending relationships. It shows us how our written expressions of emotion can become so much more than we imagined. Ruth's father turned that letter into a healing legacy. And each of us has the opportunity to do the same for our loved ones during the progression of life or toward the end of life. Yet we have such resistance to acknowledging when the end of life might be.

Letters of Affirmation and Good-bye

If writing letters like this can provide opportunities for healing, why would anyone resist writing them at the end of a loved one's life? Or for that matter, why would we resist simply talking with a loved one about the possibility of dying? As discussed earlier in the book, death denial is certainly a deterrent. This denial can be so strong that we overlook the most obvious indications that a loved one may not recover from a terminal illness or may not return from a dangerous journey or combat. Some of us hold out for miracles right up until a loved one's last breath. That's what I did—and I know countless others who have done the same. It would make sense that we wouldn't want to write final messages of good-bye to our loved one. We don't want them to die or to even consider this possibility, this reality. Sometimes it even feels like we can't.

The truth is we can. And most of us know that we should consider the reality and inevitability of death. But even if we realize this and agree, we still may not talk with a loved one about dying, because we don't know what to say—or even how to begin. For this we can borrow from the experience and expertise of hospice workers. One of Ira Byock's approaches to talking with his patients about death is very user friendly; it doesn't take a medical degree or clinical license to master. When he learns that a hospice patient has not yet talked about death, he simply asks a question like, Is there anything you want to talk about that you haven't yet?[18] Such an open-ended question often turns out to be just what is needed for both the patient and the family.

Borrowing from this simple approach, we can use a similar philosophy when crafting Legacy Letters of affirmation and good-bye at the end of someone's life. Below you will find some questions and reflections that may help you decide what to express in a Legacy Letter of good-bye:

- What do you admire about this person? (Think about the small and big things.)
- What are you grateful to this person for?
- What do you want to make sure this person knows? Even if you have spoken these words, go ahead and put them in writing.
- What memories do you hold dear and want to let them know you hold dear?
- What do you need to say that you haven't been able to say yet?
- What do you regret about your relationship with this person?
- What does this person need to hear as they approach the end of life?
- What might you need to ask or grant forgiveness for?
- What do you want to say again to make sure this person knows?

- Describe the legacy that this person will leave behind. (Again think, big and small.)

These questions have made it much easier for me to write letters to aging and ill family members. Sometimes what I write is short and simple, other times it's longer. It depends on what needs to be said—and heard. To further guide your writing, I have also included an outline for a Legacy Letter of good-bye in appendix 5. Similar to writing Final Words, before reading the outline I encourage you to try writing on your own first.

The need to say all there is to say to and from loved ones in the armed forces may be one of the more obvious opportunities for writing Legacy Letters. PFC Jesse Givens's letter (see chapter 1) illustrates how the written word can be used in a powerful and healing way. Such communications are both sad and satisfying. And all of us are included in this charge. Each of us will die at some point, and so will our loved ones. We all have the opportunity and responsibility to say good-bye. But more than that, writing final messages can lead to a mighty inheritance of healing. This was the case for Cindy.

When I think of Cindy's final letter of good-bye to her mother, I think of wisdom, courage, pain, and peace. Cindy was living fourteen hours away (by car) when her mother was diagnosed with terminal cancer. Cindy flew to visit her mother for a while but had to return to her young children back home much sooner than she would have liked. It is always difficult to be separated by miles when parents are ill, and deeply difficult when they are terminally ill. Back home, Cindy decided to write her mother a letter. Knowing it would be the last letter she would ever write to her mother, she chose each word carefully as she reviewed and affirmed her mother's life. I am not certain how Cindy's mother reacted to this letter; her energy declined quickly in the last month. But it was an amazing letter. I know this because Cindy read it at her mother's funeral. She read it with the power and grace of a loving daughter who wanted to affirm and honor her mother's life—and that she did.

As I sat in the church listening to the letter being read, I looked around at Cindy's family, her mother's neighbors, and long-time friends. Between sobs they were smiling and laughing. I imagine her mother felt many of these same emotions as she read the letter. It was in that moment that I understood how affirming loved ones at the end of their lives is both sad and beautiful at the same time. It must be. This is a Legacy Letter in the fullest sense.

It's All Good

There is value in communicating important life messages in written form to those we love. Whether the letter is written during the course of a loved one's life or at the end, the effect of affirmation, celebration, gratitude, and reconciliation can be healing for everyone involved. Yet final messages seem to be qualitatively different. There is something very powerful when words are intended to transcend this life and stretch across eternity. If for some reason you do not want to write a Legacy Letter of final affirmation to a loved one who may be facing the end of his or her life, I hope that the concept of creating a healing legacy may serve as the catalyst for simply writing a letter. And when it is too late to write loved ones who have already passed, perhaps you will recall—or rediscover—written corre-spondences from years ago that conveyed important messages.

You may struggle with not knowing what to say because the messages are as complex as your loved ones' lives and your relationships with them. It can also get complicated as you try to determine what type of letter is for whom and for which sit-uation. But if you set aside some time and reflect on the person's life, I believe you will figure it out. Truthfully, the types of letters and what you call them doesn't really matter. What matters most is writing them.

CHAPTER 6

WOMEN'S HERITAGE

SCIENTIFIC RESEARCH OF most types was initially conducted on men and then generalized to everyone. But over the past several decades, women have become a subject of study in their own right. There has also been an increase in research with diverse groups of women. A similar parallel can be made to world history. The lives and contributions of men have been represented for centuries, while women have not yet been fully represented by most historical accounts.

Writing Final Words and Legacy Letters is not only a form of emotional expression, but it is also an act of caregiving. Women have been granted dominance in the spheres of emotion and caregiving for ages. But caregiving has historically been ignored or devalued in favor of economic prowess, and reason has always trumped emotion. It should come as no surprise, then, that over the centuries, woman's oppression has often rendered her voiceless.

So that women might be more fully represented and heard, in this chapter I draw from research in women's studies, as well as from my experience as a woman and therapist, to explore the relationship between gender and the process of writing final messages.

Gender Glasses

What is the relationship between gender and the writing process for women? To determine this relationship, it is important to have a working understanding of gender. Susan Basow, a noted gender scholar, defines gender as the pressure to be masculine or feminine as defined by one's culture.[1] This suggests that the reason men and women look and behave differently from one another is based on their socialization. Indeed, we may all grow up in the same larger culture, but there are separate rules for males and females within this culture. Such rules pressure us to behave in masculine or feminine ways depending on our biological sex. This can result in—and perpetuate—differing gender roles and stereotypes. We often see these roles and stereotypes best when we are wearing "gender glasses," or metaphorical eyeglasses that heighten our awareness of how gender affects our thoughts, feelings, behaviors, relationships, and life choices. Gender glasses provide equal opportunity vision. For example, looking through the lens of gender we can better see the loss of women's voices as well as the loss of men's emotions.

Since men and women are socialized differently, they often have different careers, family relationships, friendships, hobbies, and clothing styles (to name a few). But another critical point is often overlooked: men and women have the same basic human needs and *they are more alike than different.*[2,3] Yet despite these inherent similarities, people seem to focus primarily on their more polarized "Mars and Venus" differences, which is very easy to do. If men and women start out life with similar psychological needs, why do we end up behaving in such different ways? Social scientists would say it is because of culture; evolutionary scientists would say it is because of biology. However, although biology contributes to some of the consistent differences between men and women, it appears that the more men and women are pressured in gendered ways, the more likely it is that they will develop different expectations, gender role behaviors, and issues. And from this a historical backdrop unfolds.

Historical Perspectives

Any thumbnail sketch of women's history cannot be adequate. The work of countless pioneers, scholars, and leaders is clearly not represented in the following paragraphs. But an overview can provide a meaningful framework for discussing the value of women's emotional and caregiving skills, which are quite relevant to the task of writing final messages For those interested in reading more about women's history, many excellent books exist.[4,5,6]

Less than one hundred years ago, women in the United States could not bequeath or receive an inheritance. Less than fifty years ago, married women in some states did not retain individual property rights. And in many countries this is still true. Today, U.S. women can write and publish. They can also include Final Words as a companion to their last will and testament to create the type of legacy they wish to leave. But this has not always been the case. And much of this has to do with women's oppression.

Despite the fact that I grew up next door to Seneca Falls, New York, the birthplace of women's suffrage, I was not truly aware of woman's role in history—or her oppression—until my late twenties. I also didn't know that the Women's Rights National Historical Park was located there (but I *did* know the location of the boys' Little League Hall of Fame, three hours away). Since it is not possible to review women's history, or the multitude of factors that affect women in part of a chapter, I focus briefly on feminism within the United States because it serves as an umbrella of women's issues. On a related note, when I introduce the term "feminist" to students in my undergraduate psychology of gender courses, I refer to it as "the other F word." I choose this hyperbole to emphasize that negative connotations regarding feminism continue to prevail. Indeed, when I ask students how many consider themselves to be feminists, only a few hands go up. But after learning that feminism means supporting equality between men and women, most decide they have been feminists all along.

The U.S. suffrage movement in the early 1900s is often referred to as the first wave of feminism. Lucretia Mott, Susan B. Anthony, Alice Paul, Sojourner Truth—these are a few of the pioneers who devoted their lives to gaining women's right to vote and the legal privileges that later resulted, including property ownership, inheriting and bequeathing inheritance, and initiating divorce. Control of their own property came slowly to married women, creeping through many acts of legislation over more than fifty years. It wasn't until state marital property laws were passed that women gained equal contractual powers and the right to control portions of the community property that they earned. This included dispersion of material possessions through the last will and testament.

Not surprisingly, other gains in women's equality were initiated during the late 1960s, also known as the second wave of feminism and the women's liberation movement. Some scholars credit Simone de Beauvoir's book *The Second Sex*,[7] and Betty Freidan's book *The Feminine Mystique*,[8] as catalysts for this second wave. De Beauvoir's work articulated and challenged the relegated status of woman to "other" in relation to men. For her part, Friedan identified the "unnamed problem"—that is, that women were depressed because they wanted to be more than "just housewives." Yet Friedan's description of women's discontent did not represent all women. Many African American women, who were cooking, cleaning, and providing childcare for the unhappy white housewives, often wanted to be at home caring for their own children and homes. Woman had indeed been erased, and in many ways this social movement made her more visible.

Women's studies as a discipline grew out of this women's movement. It developed like a web from anthropology, literature, psychology, and sociology. And it now represents the diversity of women's lives, including race, ethnicity, class, and sexual orientation. There has been speculation that feminism as a social movement is in a period of abeyance. There has also been discussion about a "third wave" of feminism.[9,10] One aspect of this third wave suggests that girls and women have found an equal place with men, whether at home or in careers, while maintaining ownership of their sexuality. (Think Madonna, not Gloria Steinem.)

Women's Issues in Context

In light of the different historical roots between men and women, it isn't surprising that they would have different issues to deal with. An examination of women's issues can provide a glimpse into matters of concern to women in various cultures. A cursory way to begin examining a topic is to look at book-shelves or conduct an Internet search. Let's see if this is true for women's issues.

A few of the thirty-two thousand books about women's issues that popped up on a recent Amazon.com search were *Women Who Love Too Much; French Women Don't Get Fat; Five Minutes to Orgasm Every Time You Make Love; Simple Abundance: A Daybook of Comfort and Joy; New Dimensions in Women's Health; Nice Girls Don't Get the Corner Office.* A Google search yielded about 24.7 million hits for "women's issues." Here is a very small sample listed in alphabetical order: anorexia; body image; breast (cancer, size, milk); bulimia; children; contraceptives; divorce; domestic violence; how to juggle work and career; hormone replacement therapy; infertility; lesbian; sexuality; sexual harassment; single moth-erhood. And finally, here are a few book titles about women from my professional bookshelf: *In Our Own Words: A History of Their Own; In a Different Voice: Psychological Theory and Women's Development; Reviving Ophelia: Saving the Selves of Adolescent Girls; Making a Difference: Psychology and the Construction of Gender; Women, Race, and Class.*

The same way an archeologist sifts through relics to piece together the story of a culture, this smattering of book titles and Internet hits tells a story, too. The books on my professional shelf reflect what was discovered almost three decades ago: women are a valid subject of study. They also suggest that gender has something to do with women's lives and place in society. By comparison, the themes of book titles and Internet hits from popular culture suggest that in addition to needing validation, women need to be fixed. Talk about mixed messages! Over time, I have observed that some of the reasons girls and women seek therapy are mirrored not only in the themes and titles I have listed, but also in the mixed messages they receive.

This glimpse into women's issues suggests that the study of women appears to be as unique as the issues they face. So as you begin to reflect on gender in the broader context of *women's lives,* a range of themes and legacies will likely emerge and guide your final messages to loved ones.

Emotional Intelligence, Women, and Writing

We could debate whether women's association with emotions has been viewed positively or negatively over the centuries. From my vantage point as a counselor and developmental psychologist, emotion is as important as cognition. Therefore, I think this association is advantageous.

Introduced in the previous chapter, emotional intelligence (EI) is a relatively new area of psychological study that has gained prominence over the past two decades. The skill set of perceiving and expressing emotion is central to writing Final Words and Legacy Letters. The ability to feel and express one's own feelings and to perceive and empathize with the feelings of others is a skill that women as a group have been allowed to have and practice more than men. Certainly some individual men or boys may be better at expressing their feelings than some women or girls, but on the whole, a group difference exists in practice and skill level.

Explanations for this gender difference range from biological to social; however, most of us tend to attribute all differences between men and women to biology. Indeed, I began my study of gender believing that the differences were biological. But after a decade of reviewing research and teaching gender courses, as well as simply observing men and women in the world around us, I have concluded that most behavioral differences have social causes. And this is especially true for emotional expression. A pivotal point for me was learning that infant boys are more emotionally expressive than infant girls.[11,12] Another was my own dissertation research, in which boys and girls reported the same levels of emotional expression in fifth grade, but by eighth grade and twelfth grade, girls reported being significantly more emotionally expressive than boys.[13,14] Although this is not an exhaustive review of research on the subject, it provides some reference points regarding gender differences in emotional expression.

Most women get lots of practice expressing both positive

and negative emotions. It is familiar terrain. But this does not necessarily translate into the notion that writing final good-byes to loved ones will be easy. Indeed, perceiving the emotional needs of the person to whom one is writing can also become a liability. It can allow much emotional pain, fear, and sadness to slip into the writing process. But since women have social permission to experience and express these emotions, it is likely that emotional regulation skills and social support have been developed over time to contain strong emotions. Simply put, woman can—and do—succeed at handling intense emotions.

With this vote of confidence, it is important to acknowledge how all girls and women are obviously not the same. Nor do they have the same lives or cultural experiences. And not all girls and women will find emotional expression and writing to be easy. Some may have followed the masculine code of emotional conduct through life: they don't talk about things that bother them, they mask feelings (especially the vulnerable ones), and they don't cry. If this describes you, and you'd like to broaden your emotional expression, it may be helpful to read the next chapter written for men. It addresses how to untie the masculine straitjacket that often restricts emotional expression. Skim through and take what you need. Many women are affected by masculine socialization and for good reason. Though socialized by many feminine gender roles and stereotypes, the larger mainstream culture is patriarchal and masculine. Just like their male counterparts, girls and women adapt in order to compete and succeed.

One Woman's Final Words

The letter my great-aunt Mary wrote on her deathbed is the story of a woman's life in context. It integrates much of what has been discussed thus far in the chapter and also illustrates how writing final messages is almost natural when someone accepts the reality of death and realizes how leaving words to loved ones can comfort and guide them when we are gone. As a child, I was mesmerized by my great-aunt Mary's story. When I recently asked my mother to retell the story, I listened just as eagerly as when I was a seven-year-old girl.

Measured by today's standards, Mary would have been an independent career woman who remained single. But for a woman who came of age in the late 1800s, such a lifestyle concerned Mary's parents. Their efforts to persuade her to adopt an "appropriate" life for a young woman during the Victorian period were not successful. And worse, her parents' differing opinions only served to distance Mary further from them. This detachment included resisting her parents' invitations to return to church.

Mary contracted tuberculosis in her twenties while working as a nurse in New York City. When it became clear that she would not recover, she returned to her faith. As a child, Mary had a special devotion to Saint Theresa, who is often referred to as the Little Flower because of her promise to send roses as a sign of intercession. Her "little way" to holiness was especially popular with ordinary people, because she modeled an example of achieving sanctity through small acts of great kindness. So Mary prayed to Saint Theresa of Lisieux for strength at the end of her life. And like the parable of the lost sheep,

Mary learned that she was welcomed back into the fold, even on her deathbed.

This story could be considered miraculous merely in terms of conversion. When a heart of stone becomes warm and loving after prayer, it would seem to be no less than divine intervention. I see this now. But that idea was lost on me as a child. What drew me in and shaped my own faith journey was an apparent miracle involving flowers. You see, moments after Mary died, her hospital room became filled with the smell of roses. But there were no flowers in her room, the room next door, or in the hallway. The attending medical staff had no explanation. But Mary's mother knew what had happened. And when I heard the story for the first time, even as a young child, I knew, too. *God really does exist.* I still remember where I was sitting. I recall how the long slant of evening shadows stretched out before me across the front yard. I also remember my mother's matter-of-fact way of telling the story. Being an adult, she had long ago figured out such things. Her equanimity didn't diminish my newly discovered joy, though, and my heart grew.

Having renewed her faith just before she died, Mary must have been moved to write a good-bye letter to her family. I did not realize that my mother had the original letter until we sat down during a recent visit to look through photo albums of my mother's early life. I had never seen these pictures before. Like so many women of that time, her life as *a person* ended when motherhood began. One could argue that this is still true; today's women may have traded their working-mother distress for the previous generation's stay-at-home ennui. So not only was I thrilled to get to know my mother as she was (before I knew her), but it was also this intimate sharing that produced the letter from my great-aunt Mary. The yellowed handwritten sheets of paper were taped securely between the pages of my mother's photo album. Here is an excerpt of the letter:

To My Family,

Mother dear, you who cared for me helped me and loved me . . . perhaps now you can have a little rest and I do wish you could have a few of the things of the world that will make you happy, such as we talked of the night I told you I thought the "Little Flower" heard me. I am writing this because I think I shall soon see her.

As Esther's [Mary's sister] children get old enough to understand, please tell them to listen to the voice that directs them when they are in doubt.

To Margie, but mostly Kathryn [other sisters] be more considerate of Momma. She worries over you. She won't be with you much longer, so appreciate while you have her. Do not think her ideas old-fashioned. They are not and if you obey her you will save yourself much unhappiness and misery. As I am writing this on my death-bed I say to you if I had always followed my mother's advice, I could die happier knowing I had not been a source of worry to her. She was always right but I did not see it until too late.

The ending of the letter included more personal statements and wishes. Oddly, unless a final page was missing, it wasn't signed. As I reflect on Mary's letter with great care, I realize it is the story of another person's life, and I do not want to project my views onto hers. Yet several caregiving themes appear to emerge: concern for those left behind, expression of affection, and sharing life lessons so others would learn from mistakes. Despite the fact that Mary may have led a life that she wanted to, her final letter reveals that she also regretted the way these choices may have negatively affected family relationships. Thus, her letter almost has a pleading tone as she advises siblings, nieces, and nephews to listen to their parents —and especially to that small voice inside that *directs when in doubt.*

Mary's letter is also an example of Final Words, since it was intended to be read after her death. But this letter could have been written at any time. I find myself wondering whether Mary and her parents would have enjoyed an earlier reconciliation if she had written a Legacy Letter earlier in her life to express love, gratitude, or forgiveness. Perhaps Mary's final message extends beyond her family to us.

Women as Caregivers

Though my great-aunt Mary chose the caregiving profession of nursing, she did not adopt the role of caregiver within a family. Yet it is clear that her final messages were spoken from the heart of a caregiver. Indeed, writing Final Words and Legacy Letters is an act not only of emotional expression but also of caregiving. Nurturing the emotional needs of other people would be considered caregiving, as is taking care of domestic needs such as shopping, cooking, and cleaning.

Child care is also considered caregiving behavior, along with driving a car pool of kids from one activity to another. One who engages in these behaviors would be considered a "caregiver." In hospice work, the family member or loved one who provides daily medical, physical, and emotional support to terminally ill people is also referred to as a caregiver.

Women don't formally study caregiving and don't get certified in it, but somewhere along the way they learn it is an expected gender role, and they learn how to do it. Due to the doctrine of separate spheres in most societies, this role has been delegated and embraced by women for centuries (perhaps millennia). This becomes especially true as a culture shifts from agrarian to industrial—that is, when men stop working the land near home and go into the public domain while women continue to work within the home. Indeed, most caregiving responsibilities occur behind house walls, rendering them invisible.

In contemporary industrialized cultures, even though most women now also leave home to work, they are still primarily charged with family and hearth, or the "second shift," a term coined by sociologist Arlie Hochschild. This term refers to how women continue to carry the lion's share of unpaid domestic work in dual-income families. Hochschild's research indicated that women work an additional fifteen hours per week in their second shift, translating to approximately an extra month of twenty-four-hour days per year.[15] Other scholars and researchers find this pattern is still present in the beginning of the twenty-first century. Though men took on more responsibilities for housework during the late 1990s, women are still most responsible for child care.[16] Indeed, for every hour a father spends taking care of a young child, a mother spends three hours doing so.[17]

I include observations about gender and caregiving not to call attention to men's need to do more at home. Rather I want to point out that caregiving is a familiar activity for women. And the writing of Final Words or Legacy Letters can be considered one of the purest acts of caregiving. Women and girls learn early and often that they should pay attention to the needs and feelings of others. So in some ways, thinking about loved ones who will be left behind is a natural caregiving behavior for women. But caregiving can become a double-edged sword if it crosses boundaries that interfere with women's own emotional and personal care.

To be healthy, a caregiver must remain a person with needs of her own as she engages in caregiving behaviors. Her needs must be recognized and honored by her as well as by others. So when writing Final Words and Legacy Letters, it is important for women to know where their needs end and where those of others begin. This is referred to as having "healthy boundaries" in psychotherapy, and it becomes relevant when writing final messages because it is time to say what one truly wants and needs to say.

Writing Final Words and Legacy Letters to Loved Ones

The preceding information was intended to orient you to broader issues surrounding women's lives and to prepare you for the actual writing process. Some of the significant relationships in women's lives are addressed below, along with

perspectives and suggestions about how to honor those relationships with Final Words and Legacy Letters.

Parents

There are two basic options when writing Final Words and
Legacy Letters to parents: write to them as a couple, or write to
them individually. I don't have a general recommendation
about which is better, as this is a personal decision that depends
on your relationship with them. Only you know which feels
right. If you choose to write to each parent individually, you
will be essentially reflecting on a mother-child and father-child
relationship. This can open old wounds as well as heal them. It
can stir up resentment as well as bring forgiveness.

When writing Final Words or Legacy Letters, most parents
need to know that they are loved by their children. Most parents also need to know that they are forgiven for the ways they
have hurt or disappointed their children, intentionally or not.
As you reflect on this, it is important to remember that every
parent hurts or disappoints their child in some way. Despite
my best efforts and good intentions, I know that I have hurt
and disappointed my children at some point and wish that
this could be changed. Yet some of the most penetrating
moments of compassion in my life have been when my children simply said, "I forgive you, Mom," or, "It's okay, Mom."
So as you reflect on your relationship with your parents, please
keep in mind their need to be forgiven. And if you need to ask
forgiveness from them, Final Words and Legacy Letters provide a way to initiate your request. Hearts can be softened at
any point in time.

There are other aspects of the relationship with your parents that you may want to include in your final messages. Parents need to know that what they did mattered in life—their work, their sacrifices, and their intentions. Sometimes parents weren't the best parents we wanted them or needed them to be. But almost every parent I have worked with in counseling, regardless of their harmful or neglectful behavior, was doing the best they could. I recall a mother who constantly scrutinized her four-year-old daughter's weight—so much so that this little girl (who did not have a weight problem) was hiding food in her desk drawer so she could enjoy it when her mother wasn't watching. This mother's behavior might seem unreasonable, but her intention was not. She had struggled with a weight problem most of her life and just wanted to prevent her daughter from the same difficulty.

A special note about Final Words and Legacy Letters with the mother-daughter and father-daughter relationships: each of these relationships is complex, to say the least. And whole chapters and books have been written about such relationships (along with songs, movies, etc.). What I hope to convey is how very important it is to honestly reflect on your relationship with your mother and father. Perfect children and perfect parents don't exist. This perspective develops over time and is an antidote to egocentric narcissism that can turn any parent into a villain.

I decided to give my mother a letter of affirmation and final legacy when she was in her early eighties. After several bouts with cancer, the disease appeared to be in remission. I had written Final Words to her and felt at peace that nothing was left unsaid. Then I started thinking, *What if she died first?* In the absence of a fatal accident of some type for me, this was much more likely. Since my mother knew I was working on this book, I asked if I could send some personal final messages while we were both still alive. She said yes without hesitation. This is how the idea of writing Legacy Letters to elderly loved ones was born.

Not everyone will need to seek permission to give their parent such a letter. But I knew it would be emotional and I didn't want to surprise my mother. As previously mentioned, I had written her a letter of gratitude when I first became a mother, so I thought this would be easy. But writing this second letter was very different. It was a retrospective of her life and our relationship; it acknowledged her mortality from that eternity perspective. It was especially challenging because I would be accountable for anything I expressed, since we would both be alive after she read it. I didn't want to insult either one of us by sugarcoating our lives; and I didn't want to reopen any wounds that had long since healed. I ended up with my usual recipe: I said a prayer, asked for guidance, and wrote from my heart. The letter had a wistful tone of *I want to make sure you know . . .* The core theme was gratitude and recognition of a lifetime she devoted to caregiving. Her courage and faith through many challenges in life were also affirmed. The letter expressed many of the things that I would have said if I were to speak at her funeral.

My mother was grateful for this Legacy Letter. She said that it took more than a day to finish reading; she kept putting it down because she kept crying—with joy. It truly was a legacy for her. And I felt at peace knowing that nothing had been left unsaid.

Stepparents

Your Final Words and Legacy Letters to stepparents will reflect the quality of closeness and the nature of the relationship you had with them. For some, the relationship will more closely resemble a parent-child relationship, and thus your messages will be written more like those to a biological parent. For others, the relationship may have been distant or even negative. If this is the case, you always have the option of not writing final messages. But in my experience as a counselor and advocate of written emotional expression, there are surprisingly wonderful benefits when we try to complete our unfinished business. It may not result in immediate drastic changes, but it can shine a light into our shadows where healing and wholeness are waiting to be found.

Husband or Partner

Writing Final Words or Legacy Letters to the person with whom you have chosen to eat, sleep, pray, fight with, and make love to most of your life is not a small thing. I described part of my experience writing to my husband in chapter 4. You will soon have your own experience to reflect upon and perhaps even share with others. Be prepared for overwhelming gratitude, sadness, and finality—each in the purest sense. Also be prepared for the possibility of improvements in certain aspects of your relationship.

In many ways, writing these words will be like writing to

anyone else. You will reflect upon and review the relationship, express or ask for forgiveness, and convey life lessons, regrets, or hopes. You will express what is wonderful about this person. But what makes this final message different is the possibility that once your spouse or partner's life resembles some type of normality in the future, they could remarry or become committed romantically to someone else. This concept can be impossible to fathom for some; many women may expect or want to remain connected to their spouse or partner through eternity. This is normal and okay. But if you can give the blessing of freedom to enter future relationships, make a statement about it in your Final Words. If you can't bring yourself to do this, then it is probably best not to say anything at all and let the future be in your partner's hands.

Friends

Over the course of life, women develop many different types of friendships. They have friends from high school, college, graduate or professional school, jobs, boards, work, book clubs, sports teams, community clubs and projects, and so forth. When deciding which friends to whom you will give a final message, the following suggestions may guide you:

Closeness. Reflect upon your attachments. If you feel particularly attached to someone, and they to you, this is probably someone who needs a final message from you.

Need. Ask yourself if you need a final message from the friends in your life. If you do, then it is possible that they need one from you, too.

Conflict. If you have experienced any cutoffs or conflicts with friends that have not been resolved yet, you may want to write Final Words or a Legacy Letter to them, or resolve that issue face-to-face now.

Another issue to consider is how gender may affect friendships. Women are much more likely than men to have many close relationships. Certainly this is not true of all women and men, but it does reflect the different gender socialization process. This leads to a focus on "girlfriends" and "guy friends." All of us have relationships with men and women that are significant. This is true whether we are married or single. If you are single, you are perhaps freer to write to whom you wish. But if you are married, there is no need to feel as if you are betraying your current spouse if you write to a former lover or ex-spouse/partner. These are *your* Final Words and Legacy Letters. Who and what you decide to write is up to you. By the time women reach middle age, there have been many opportunities to resolve any unfinished business. But if that hasn't happened, you can still make it happen with Final Words or Legacy Letters.

Ex-spouses and Ex-partners

You may or may not have something left to say to a former spouse or partner. Given enough chances and courage, people can get healthy closure with one another after a committed relationship ends. But we know that this is not always the case. Final Words and Legacy Letters are very appropriate—perhaps even needed—when former spouses and partners still experience conflict and resentment due to infidelity and betrayal. The betrayal may have taken on the form of an affair, chronic illness, unemployment, or a career decision. Marriages and unions can end, but unhealthy soul ties will last forever until they are cut. Legacy Letters and Final Words offer a way to explore—or express—forgiveness and to be free.

Concluding Thoughts for Women

The process of writing intimate letters is likely a familiar task for women. Indeed, many women grew up writing love letters to their best friends as well as to family members. Because of this practice, women may bring an established skill set to writing intimate and emotional messages. Yet as they do this, it is important for women to express themselves fully, without social or historical constraints that can silence them. As a result of almost three decades of scholarship in women's studies and the psychology of women, there is a greater understanding both of woman's nature and her oppression. While many outcomes may occur as a result of writing final messages, the healing that can occur extends far beyond gender roles and stereotypes. Women can now bequeath both their material *and* emotional inheritance. Let this legacy and the power of the written word speak for itself.

꧁ CHAPTER **7** ꧂

MEN'S HERITAGE

I WAS AT a social gathering when a friend made an announce-
ment about me without checking first, "I want you all to
know that Mary just published a book about boys!" I have
always felt uncomfortable being the center of attention, so I
forced a smile and waited for everyone to go back to what they
were doing. But they didn't. All eyes were on me as I began
answering questions about the title *(Boy Talk),* the topic (boys'
emotional expression), and details about the writing process.
Just as the spotlight was finally fading, another question shot
out. It was Jimmy DiGiacomo, an adult with sons of his own
now; he had been a wild teenager who cruised around town in
a white Corvette that everyone coveted.

True to character, Jimmy goaded, "If you don't have sons

and you're not a guy, how could you write a book about boys?"
This is the kind of situation you either love or hate. As it
turned out, I was surprisingly neutral, probably because I had
fielded this question many times before. I replied quietly and
said something about my research and being a therapist.
Jimmy nodded in approval and I smiled back. Then as if on
cue, a toddler wandered into the room and started crying. The
spotlight was finally off of me.

I begin with this vignette to state the obvious—I'm not
male. Yet I have accrued knowledge about the development of
boys' and men's emotional expression through a combination
of study, research, and clinical work. So it's not so much that
I have a "right" to discuss this—as Jimmy's question
implied—but rather that I have a responsibility to discuss
challenges and benefits to the writing of Final Words and
Legacy Letters for men.

Final Words, Legacy Letters, and Men

Men have been charged with the role of "protector" in most
cultures. This has included the real and perceived expectation
that men must protect their families, their towns, and their
countries. We see this expectation expressed in gender roles and
stereotypes as well as in the division of labor. Indeed, men out-
number women in many of the careers that involve protection
—firefighting, law enforcement, the military. A common element in the role of protector, whether at home or on the job,
involves courage. But it also requires a type of dissociation
from emotional pain and vulnerability. Though obviously all
men do not work in careers that require dissociation from

feelings, the gender role expectation to "turn off" vulnerable feelings is often required "to become a man." When men take this expectation to heart, expressing feelings in final messages can seem foreign.

But writing Final Words and Legacy Letters is more than just expressing feelings. It is also about the intimate nature of relationships and how the writing process becomes a way to honor those relationships. Yet as a group, men have had much less practice—and less cultural permission—to fully express their emotional selves in relationships. Indeed, in the service of following rigid rules of hypermasculinity (i.e., boys don't cry, don't be a wimp, stay in control, dominate), men have been mandated to restrict their emotional expression, which can sometimes block intimate communication. Thus, men's first task when writing final messages to loved ones is to overcome any cultural roadblocks that get in the way.

It is not healthy to constantly repress joy and affection; it is also not healthy to always ignore sadness and grief. Left unattended for a lifetime, such feelings may seem confusing and overwhelming when they surface. But men can learn to handle them, as well as the emotional aspect of relationships. Writing Final Words and Legacy Letters is an invitation to rediscover both.

Restricted Emotional Expression: Roots in Boyhood

My husband, John Lynch, is a clinical psychologist and author who specializes in men's issues. John's work exposes him not only to the men that boys grow into, but also to the boys that remain within men. He has observed that men learn early and well to suppress their emotions. As boys, they figured out that their feelings were a liability rather than an asset in most social situations. And when these boys become men, they bring the same liability with them into adulthood. Men's interpersonal relationships and physical health can suffer as a result. Lynch contends that men's lives are often shortened, limited, and lonely when they continue following rigid rules of masculinity in adulthood.[1] I refer to these as the *pack rules*,[2] and William Pollack refers to them as the *boy code*.[3]

Reclaiming men's emotional lives is as difficult and possible as changing the way we're raising boys. In addition to, or per-haps because of these rules, Lynch also states that part of what keeps boys and men hiding emotions from one another is the "silent masculine inquisition." Inside their heads, men ask themselves, *Am I playing by the rules correctly? Am I doing it right? Am I man enough?* And because these questions are asked silently and answered subjectively, they are resistant to change. This silence girds an underlying principle of traditional masculinity: *Don't show me your vulnerability and I won't show you mine.* Boys learn quickly that their parents and the rest of their world don't expect them to express vulnerable feelings either. And if they do, there is punishment. It should come as no surprise, then, that boys and men often do not express—and often do not even feel—their emotions at all. In fact, there is a condition called *alexithymia,* translated as "without words for feelings," that refers to the inability to describe how one is feeling. The condi-tion first became identified within brain-injured patients, but it is now a focus of research and discussion within men's studies. Lynch points out that alexithymia is rarely, if ever, discussed as a condition in non-brain-injured girls or women.[4]

Results of Masculinity Rules

Although enduring the trials of rigid masculinity affects boys and men individually, it is not a unique or random experience. "Successful" masculinity becomes narrowly defined by culture in antifeminine terms. But for this definition to take effect upon men's behaviors and emotions, the entire culture must collude. And indeed it does. A recent episode of *Saturday Night Live* parodied the fear of feminizing men by advertising "Homicil," a fictional prescription to allay parents' fears when their young sons act in feminine ways (cooking, taking ballet, or playing with girls). The expectation to be rigidly masculine and avoid feminine characteristics is overtly and covertly communicated to boys. It is then maintained in many relationships —including families—and reinforced in an organized way in school, athletic, and corporate institutions. In the face of such a rigid cultural mandate, another truth must be exposed: emotions don't feminize men, they *humanize* men.

You may remember the "dysfunctional family" pattern that was identified in the 1980s. The directives in families that were labeled "dysfunctional" boiled down to: *don't feel, don't talk, and don't trust.* Simultaneously, such families outwardly projected an image of health by emphasizing performance and achievement. This is obviously not a good recipe for mental health. And if you look closely, these dysfunctional rules mirror hypermasculinity (emotional aloofness, constant competition, avoiding intimacy) and too often become the foundation for the way adult men relate to one another and their loved ones. When boys or men choose to express feelings and are ridiculed, they often choose to make the feelings go underground again. This perpetuates the vicious cycle of feeling, hiding, feeling, and hiding. The layers add up until it's hard to feel anything at all.

Repression of emotions not only can affect men's health, but it also can be lethal. A man's life expectancy continues to be nearly *seven years* less than a woman's.[5,6] To put this alarming statistic in perspective, a six-month difference would be considered significant. Men lead women in all of the fifteen leading causes of death. Men also lead women in suicide by a ratio of 4:1, and the ratio increases to 10:1 in older age ranges.[7] Between the ages of twenty-five and forty-four years old, men die of heart disease at nearly three times the rate for women.[8] We prematurely lose fathers, grandfathers, husbands, brothers, uncles, and the wisdom that comes only from our elders.

Though a single and direct cause-effect link cannot be made between men's emotional restriction and increased morbidity or mortality, current scholars in men's studies suggest the link is there. A basic finding in men's health studies is that the more a man adheres to the attitudes and demands of narrowly defined masculinity, the more he is at risk for health problems.[9,10] Emotion researchers are finding that the suppression of both negative and positive emotions can also affect cognitive thinking.[11,12] But the problems associated with narrowly defined masculinity don't end there. Men also exhibit violent behaviors, alcoholism, and risk-taking behaviors that can interfere with intimate relationships. And when intimate relationships suffer, men's social support—a protective factor for health—is compromised.

Over the years, it has become evident that fathers are distant because they don't know what to do with the *emotional* part of being in a family—a central part of family life. If men didn't practice emotional and nurturing skills when they were boys, and if they weren't taught how to express anger without being aggressive, then it comes as no surprise that many fathers lack healthy emotional and relational skills in their own families.

Broadening Masculinity to Include Final Messages

Writing Final Words and Legacy Letters requires the emotional intelligence skill of emotional expression, as discussed in previous chapters. When mainstream culture does not support the emotional lives of boys and men, it only makes sense that facing feelings about one's own death could be foreign, disorienting, or overwhelming for them. Similarly, it stands to reason that empathizing with the anticipated grief of loved ones would be difficult for those who long ago were taught to turn off their emotions. With this lack of emotional skill development, writing Final Words and Legacy Letters may be difficult. Yet while men may not have developed a fluent language for emotional expression, it is absolutely possible to develop this skill set. In fact, it may even help men rediscover a long-lost emotional world.

When Terrance Real, author of the popular book about male depression *I Don't Want to Talk About It,* conducted research about masculinity in other cultures, he asked the question, What makes a "good" man?[13] One response by an African tribal leader was that a good man laughs, weeps, and protects, and does each when needed. This response suggests that it is possible to both have and show emotions and still be a man. Yet this is not always so easy, as was the case for Lee, a middle-aged hospice patient dying of lung and brain cancer.

Ira Byock tells the story of Lee in his book *Dying Well*.[14] Though the end of Lee's life was extremely sad, the only emotion he could show was anger. And he did this primarily through sarcasm and verbal aggression toward the people he loved most—his wife and children. Two months before Lee died, Dr. Byock had to commit Lee to a psychiatric ward, because his anger was becoming violent and dangerous. During the week he was hospitalized, Lee faced deep and hidden feelings from childhood for the first time. This allowed him to move beyond his defensive anger to feel his present sadness and grief. Though it was extremely difficult and foreign to do this emotional work, Lee also finally experienced some healing, and so did his family. Indeed, healing is a common outcome when men are able to face vulnerable emotions like grief, fear, or sadness.

A hospital stay is not necessary to deal with emotions. Most men and boys find out that they can handle their emotions and don't need to make them disappear or come out "sideways" in the form of other emotions or behaviors. In fact, a good way to prevent sideways emotions is to pay attention to what's going on inside: *How do I feel? What am I thinking? What happened before I felt this way?* When this is difficult to access directly, men can notice the behaviors that family and friends bring to their attention. Sometimes this feedback is difficult to ignore. ("Daddy, why are you screaming at me?" or

"Jim, I've noticed you drink or get high every time you get upset.") So if men miss the initial emotion, they can backtrack to find the initial triggers.

Whether it is a positive or negative emotion, the best way to keep it from disappearing or coming out sideways is to notice it, experience it, and express it. It is wonderful to be able to disclose important thoughts and feelings to a trusted person. But the most essential part is being able to *tell yourself.* This can be accomplished through introspection, reflective writing, and the arts (poetry, music, painting, etc.). If boys and men don't learn about healthy emotional expression in their families or from school, the other main source is through friendships and intimate relationships. When that doesn't happen, another means for rediscovering emotions is through counseling. I wish there weren't such a stigma associated with seeking counseling, because everyone—both men and women—could benefit from having a professionally trained and nonjudgmental listener on an ongoing basis.

Gender Research and Emotional Expression

Since writing Final Words and Legacy Letters involves accessing one's feelings and being able to express them, it makes sense to review some research surrounding masculinity and the development of emotional expression. Recent scientific attention has been given to the role of emotions in psychology and neuroscience,[15] and new research suggests that expressing emotion in positive and healthy ways is related to emotional and physical health.[16,17,18]

I have been teaching undergraduate courses related to the

psychology of gender for the past ten years. Most people learn about sex and gender through mass media such as TV shows, movies, news, popular magazines, and so on. However, some colleges offer gender courses where students get their first real glimpse of the complexity of gender. They also discover how gender differences can be sensationalized in mass media. Indeed, when certain scientific criteria for analyzing gender differences are neglected, misinformation can occur [19], as illustrated in the following true story.

Several years ago, the lead story on the local noon news was "Research Finds Differences in Men's and Women's Emotions Stems from Brain Difference." At this point in my own study of gender, I believed that the behavioral differences between men and women were biologically based. So I eagerly called the newsroom to get more information. I eventually tracked down the study in *Science* magazine and was surprised by what I found. The actual study stated that the "brains of men and women are fundamentally more similar than different," and only three regions of the brain showed slight processing differences in this sample of sixty-one adult men and women.[20] It's unnerving to think about the number of viewers who only heard the media bite and did not get the rest of the story. And this is only one example of misinformation.

On a related note, since this *is* only one study, it is important to state that other research (and reports of research) claims that men's brains differ from women's brains due to testosterone. Michael Gurian writes frequently about sex differences in the brain.[21] Not only do I encourage readers to carefully read the primary sources of research, as just illustrated, but I also encourage them to think about alternate explanations for certain findings, especially where brain development is concerned. It is common knowledge that the brain is "plastic," or very amenable to developmental growth and change based on stimulation and experience. For example, the brain activity of children who learn to play musical instruments looks different from children who do not. Following this logic, if men's brains structurally or functionally process emotions differently than women's, how can it be determined whether this is an innate sex difference or the effect of diminished learning and practice?

People are often surprised to learn that infants feel and express emotions.[22] People are even more surprised to learn that boys, as a group, are more emotionally expressive than infant girls. By age two, boys are less verbally expressive than girls; by age four, they are less facially expressive than girls; and by age three, they show less empathy than girls.[23, 24] (This shift toward emotional nonexpression runs counter to the typical expectation most of us have that developmental skills will improve with age. Results from my own dissertation research further expose this atypical pattern of development in emotional expression. Boys and girls reported the same levels of emotional expression in fifth grade, but by eighth grade and twelfth grade, boys reported being significantly less emotionally expressive than girls.[25] As part of this same study, boys and girls were asked to respond to the following question in writing: "Is it easy or hard to tell your feelings to someone? Tell why." Results mirrored the same gender difference in emotional expression. Also interesting was how the actual *number* of words written by boys was much less than the number written by girls.[26]

Taken together, results from this research overview suggest that the socialization of emotional expression can be influenced by gendered, cultural rules for display. This is both bad and good. The bad news is that it happens at all; boys and men should not have to turn off or "straitjacket" the expression of emotions. The good news is that if repressing emotions is a learned behavior, it can be unlearned—which leads to the task at hand. In the following interview, we see how one man moved beyond cultural influences that have restricted his emotional language so that he could write final messages to his loved ones. His struggles and solution are clearly described.

Writing Reflections: One Man's Experience

When I asked my friend Joe, a middle-aged teacher, to discuss his experience with writing final messages, he was eager to talk, since he had been struck by the concept. He also wanted to reflect on letters he had written to his mother and father earlier in his life. The correspondences eventually served as Legacy Letters, though he didn't refer to them in this way at the time. Our discussion revealed echoes of how the rules of masking emotions initially affected Joe, and how as he persevered with the reflection process, he was able to overcome this.

Joe said that he found it difficult to begin writing his Final Words. When I asked him why, he replied,

> Writing final messages involves relationships and feelings, and
> men's language is more about thinking than feeling. When I got

started, I realized it wasn't my turf. I felt daunted by the task. I kept second-guessing my words . . . Were they articulate enough? How would they compare to my wife's message to me? As I began writing Final Words to her, I started to recant the history of our relationship and realized it wasn't going how I wanted it to. I kept getting lost in the details, and the more I kept focusing on details, the further off track I got. I wanted to see the bigger picture but couldn't.

Since I knew Joe had overcome this initial obstacle, I asked him how he did it. He said that he had to "ignore comparisons and my own fear of inadequacy at being able to do this emotional work. I also put it down for a while and took a step back to see the larger picture."

I then asked Joe what happened after he took a step back. He waited a few seconds before answering, "When writing to my wife, I realized there was even more to our relationship than I had realized. And everything changed when I got this perspective. I saw that all parts of our relationship were needed . . . all the troubles and joys taken together comprised a lifetime of passages we shared . . . our journey. The perspective of writing a final message changed everything in the moment."

Joe had also written to his children and he said that the main message was to thank them for the time they had shared and what their love brought to his life. He also said that writing to his children was bittersweet, "As I thought about my kids without their dad, without that protection and connection, I felt sad. But I also became more aware of the time I have with them now and how special it is."

This led to a general discussion about the benefits of writing Final Words. Joe described an immediate benefit to his marriage, "My marriage became clearer, more evident. It put conflicts in perspective and brought an ease to arguments . . . it became easier to see my wife more in the flow of our life together, what it has been about . . . I have a different perspective." Joe said that one of the benefits that came from writing to his children was coming to terms with not being a perfect parent and wanting to work on those deficiencies. He also said, "Writing to my children also made me aware of a desire to write my brothers and sisters."

Since Joe had also written Legacy Letters to both of his parents, I asked him to comment on this experience. He said that he wrote to each of his parents for different reasons. He wrote to his mother when she was dying, because he wanted to affirm her life, as she had struggled with feeling like she had not done enough or done it well. Joe read an excerpt from the letter (his mother had saved it and told him she had often read it), which he found while going through her things after her death:

> You were always there to care, provide, help, love and transport. Our friends have known your open arms, full plates, and spare beds. . . . Your strength and goodness have come from within you and reflect your heart, soul, spirit and character. Life has not always been kind or helpful to you. People around you have not always been fair or supportive of you. But you became you anyway. You reflect the character, heart, loyalty, and integrity that you do because that is what you made of your life.

When I asked Joe about the letter to his father, he said that he wrote it in his mid-twenties and that it was about his own healing as much as his father's. He said he had wanted to try to look beyond the normal adolescent restrictions and fights: "I was trying to get out of my role as a son and trying to understand the intentions behind his behavior. I was letting him know that I understood." Since this type of letter is written while both people are alive and there is no eminent final parting, I was curious about how the two men acted after the letter was read. Joe said that he felt like he had to live up to the words he expressed to his father, that he had more accountability. As for his father's response, Joe couldn't remember. He said that his father probably didn't say much at the time, but that whatever his reaction was, it didn't take away from the letter. Joe knew it was the right thing to do.

Joe recently asked his father if he remembered the letter. It is one of a few things his father keeps in a safe deposit box.

Writing Final Messages to Loved Ones

The following sections offer information and suggestions about writing to loved ones. The information can be applied to individual or group Final Words, as well as to Legacy Letters. The intent is to provide points of reflection for the different relationships in your life. If you read this chapter and you still have difficulty writing, that's okay. You can walk away from it for a while, to let your thoughts or feelings germinate, and come back later. Also remember there are outlines for writing Final Words and Legacy Letters in the appendix section. Many of the stem sentences may help you get started. If you're still struggling, I recommend attending a workshop or contacting a friend or colleague who can coach you. It doesn't have to be done alone.

Parents

You may or may not have had a good relationship with your parents. The relationships men have with their mothers and fathers are usually as complex as the individual people in those relationships. Reasons for this vary. Yet a common family pattern that emerges time and time again includes an emotionally available mother and an emotionally distant father. One reason for this particular pattern involves cultural gender roles. While communication may exist between a mother and her son, far too many men have reflected that they really never *knew* their father, and if they did, it happened toward the end of his life. So if both of your parents are still living, you may find that it is easier, or at least more familiar, to convey intimate messages to your mother.

The ideas presented here give you several ways to leave nothing unsaid to your parents. Writing Final Words takes care of a sudden or expected death in the sense that your parents will read them after you have died. However, since most parents die before their children, you will want to consider writing a Legacy Letter as they age or if they become terminally ill. This letter of affirmation can validate their life experiences and achievements, while also expressing gratitude or addressing any areas of apology or forgiveness. Such a letter also acknowledges there will be fewer opportunities to express these thoughts and feelings, so it has a summative and final tone. If you do not want to wait until your parents are elderly or ill, you can simply write a Legacy Letter to express gratitude and to honor them. Similar issues will arise whether you are writing Final Words or Legacy Letters.

If your parents' behavior was harmful and hurtful, it can be difficult to say anything positive to them. This is not unique to men. I address such issues in chapter 9, but here it is important to generally recognize that we all have something important to say to our parents, even if they didn't give us what we needed. It might simply be, "I regret how we never had the type of relationship I wanted and needed. I understand (or don't understand) why. I just want you to know that I have a good life now and that I forgive you for not being the parent I needed." It is also possible that tension may exist between you and your parents as a result of hurtful responses to behavior. Your writing can simply reflect this truth as well as your accountability. And if you need to be forgiven by them, Final Words and Legacy Letters provide a way to initiate this.

Although some parents may be intentionally mean or spiteful, I have observed that positive intent can lie beneath some of parents' most egregious behavior. I recall Chuck, a large, muscular father who came to me for counseling. He had been charged with child abuse after leaving bruises all over his small seven-year-old son. When we began talking, Chuck revealed how his own father often beat him in the same way. Rather than cry or express rage, Chuck said that such beatings were the best thing that ever happened to him, because they kept him in line. As I began working with this family, it was necessary for me to recognize the positive intention behind this generational pattern of discipline. Both Chuck and his father did what they thought was right, and neither could learn (or teach) what they had not been shown by their own fathers. I, of course, helped Chuck find other ways to discipline his little boy. I share this example to suggest that expressing gratitude to parents can be very challenging. But if you look closely enough, the underlying intentions may have been positive, and your gratitude can then be sincere.

Another factor to consider when writing Final Words and Legacy Letters to your parents is whether to write to them jointly or individually. This is a decision you can make ahead of time based on your relationship with them. Only you know what works best for you and your family. But if you sit down and start writing a joint letter and end up being at a loss for words or realize that you are primarily writing to one parent, it would probably be best to write two separate letters. The main goal is to write in a way that allows the unique stories and relationships to emerge, to be heard, and to be honored. Though I have a preference for writing individual final messages, both group and individual formats can accomplish this goal.

Stepparents

The type of relationship you have with a stepparent will guide the content of your Final Words and Legacy Letters. It will also guide whether you even decide to write. Some men have very close relationships with their stepparents, and thus the narrative will likely follow the same themes expressed to their parents. The closeness with a stepparent is often defined by the age your parent remarried, the circumstances surrounding the remarriage, and how well your family blended. When both parents are still living, the relationship that has developed with a stepmother or stepfather may or may not be as close. I have a friend who is much closer to his stepmother than to his mother. There are no other specific guidelines about writing to stepparents. You know best whether and how to honor relationships with your stepparents.

Wife or Partner

Writing final messages to the person with whom you have chosen to spend your life, who knows your strengths and weaknesses better than anyone else, drives you nuts, has hurt or disappointed you, and has slept and made love with you is a daunting task. It can be even more challenging if there has been tension or resentment between the two of you resulting from an affair, chronic illness, unemployment, a demanding career, or another type of major hurt or disappointment. If this is the case, it will be important to acknowledge these feelings to yourself before sitting down to write. At some level, your spouse or partner is aware of this resentment. Acknowledging it may help you begin to move beyond resentment and anger toward recognizing what else is in the relationship that merits honor and appreciation.

Forgiveness is a real issue that goes both ways in relationships. If you have a need to forgive or be forgiven, make that need clear in your Final Words or Legacy Letters. Don't leave it out unless you honestly cannot forgive or be forgiven. And if that is the case, you may want to talk with someone who can help you examine the issue. Reading books published on the topic of forgiveness can also be helpful.

A specific concern that you may want to address in your Final Words involves the reality that your surviving wife or partner will have the opportunity to become involved in another romantic relationship after you are gone. This is not a small or easy topic to deal with. If you wish to give specific permission to enter a future relationship, please do. If you cannot grant this freedom or if you are unsure, you can simply write in such a way that you honor the relationship the two of you had and not speak about future relationships. This is a very personal matter, and how you handle it is up to you. I bring it to your attention so you can decide whether or not you wish to address it in your Final Words.

Friends

Friendships that feel more like family may merit a healing legacy. It makes sense that you would want to write to men and women with whom you feel attached to in some way. Similarly, it makes sense that you may not need to write final messages to fishing or drinking buddies. Nevertheless, leaving Final Words to buddies like this might be meaningful and helpful to them, especially if you have known each other throughout life. When deciding to which friends you would like to leave a final message, the following suggestions may guide you.

Closeness. Reflect upon your attachments. If you feel particularly attached to someone, and they to you, this is probably someone who needs a final message from you.

Need. Ask yourself if you need a final message from the friends in your life. If you do, then it is possible that they need one from you, too.

Conflict. If you have experienced any cutoffs or conflicts with friends that have not been resolved yet, you may want to write Final Words or a Legacy Letter to them or resolve that issue face-to-face now.

Friendships with guys are often based in activities such as playing sports, video games, and watching sports together. Activity-based relationships often don't leave much room for talking or sharing intimate thoughts and feelings, though bonding may indeed still occur. My husband has a good friend, Jim, and the two of them run together on a regular basis. When they run, they talk about a lot of subjects, and afterward they always seem happier and less stressed. A couple of years ago my husband sprained his ankle, and I wondered if they would still get together and talk regularly even if they weren't running. They didn't. By contrast, it's normal for my female friends and me to pick up the phone or e-mail each other just to talk; we don't rely on an activity to bring us together.

I point out this social gender difference as a real-life example of research that was discussed earlier in this chapter— that women are granted more social freedom than men to seek intimate conversations with one another. Thus, men are less likely to have expressed admiration, gratitude, or love to their male friends. The same applies to men's friendships with women. Writing Final Words and Legacy Letters is one way to express what may have gone unsaid thus far in friendships. And as mentioned earlier, the process of writing may also prompt new discussions in the here and now.

Ex-spouses or Ex-partners

Over the course of a lifetime, people have many chances to obtain healthy emotional closure with one another. Whether we take those chances or have enough courage is another matter. I think that Final Words and Legacy Letters are very appropriate—perhaps even needed—when former spouses and partners still experience conflict and resentment. The relationship may have ended as a result of past infidelity, betrayal, or disappointments that stem from chronic illness, or unemployment and career decisions. This can contribute to a lack of forgiveness, which often creates an unhealthy soul tie. Marriages and unions can end, but unhealthy ties last until we cut them. Forgiveness allows people to really move on. And writing Final Words and Legacy Letters is one way to set you both free.

Concluding Thoughts for Men

Men receive overt and covert messages about "how to be a man." Depending on their cultural heritage and family values, it is likely that men's intimate and vulnerable emotions were somehow punished or frowned upon when they were younger. Thus, for many men the type of reflection and emotional expression required for writing Final Words and Legacy Letters may seem like a foreign language. Some of the information in this chapter may help explain how and why such difficulties can occur. But more than that, I hope the information helps men develop some of the necessary skills for conveying final intimate messages to their loved ones. I also hope that the stories and voices of men in this book will begin to replace *the silent masculine inquisition,* so that men—and their loved ones—can reap the benefits of men's emotional expression in Final Words and Legacy Letters. As men broaden their own definition of masculinity to include all types of emotional expression, they will have better access to the emotional world. And that is another important heritage for men to bequeath.

CHAPTER 8

PARENT LEGACIES

BEFORE WRITING FINAL Words, I had another way of ensuring my children had some kind of closure and personal legacy in case I died while they were young. Here's what I did: when embarking on a trip that involved higher than normal risk, such as traveling long distances or flying, I would tell them, "I love you so much, and I'm so glad that you're my daughters. If anything were to happen to me, I'll ask God to send me back so I can be your guardian angel." Their response wasn't sad or anxious. They simply agreed it was a good idea, hugged me good-bye, and then went back to what they were doing. And I was on my way.

The first time our whole family took a plane trip together, I realized that this little ritual needed some adaptation. So I suggested that if something happened and we all died together, we would meet at a designated spot in heaven. Since none of us had ever been there and we didn't know where things were—as my then seven-year-old pointed out—she changed the meeting place. Instead, we would meet on the roof of our house. Her new rendezvous and the family's wholehearted support suggested that the idea of talking about death in our family had successfully been introduced.

Please don't think that we are always talking about death in our family (we aren't) or that my children are entirely comfortable with it (they aren't). My reason for sharing these family stories is to say that having studied lifespan development has helped me understand people at different ages. Such developmental perspectives can be important when writing final messages to young or adult children, as well as when discussing death with them. So I begin this chapter by providing a developmental framework for understanding children's cognitive and emotional development. This is followed by information on adult development.

Developmental Perspectives

The tone and content of Final Words and Legacy Letters will vary according to your children's ages. Although child development information is much more available today, when parents try to communicate with children, they often speak to children as though they are small adults. I call this *telescoping*, or seeing children as if they are more grown up than they are. (It is so easy to do, and I'm as guilty as anyone else.)

An example of telescoping involves Jason, a three-year-old boy who frequently leaves his toys in the middle of the floor. Despite his parents' repeated verbal directives not to do so, he usually forgets. This is developmentally expected, of course, but his parents still become very angry based on expectations of *adult* behavior —in other words, (most) adults don't leave things in the middle of the floor. Yet the younger brain functions with selective attention and sequential memory. This is why experts advise parents to first make sure their young children are paying attention and then give only one direction at a time. So when Jason's parents sound irritated as they tell him to pick up his toys (a third time) and come to dinner, Jason's focus is solely on getting to dinner, not the toys he steps over on the way to the kitchen.

Parents can telescope their children at any age through adulthood. This relates to writing Final Words in several ways. A telescoped adult view would be right on target for parents who write a single final message to their children rather than updating it as their children get older. Important legacies from parents will be read more often during a child's adulthood, so this telescoped vision would be accurate for later reading. But for parents who want their children to receive a final message written at younger developmental levels, word choice and content would not reflect an adult's perspective and developmental information would be helpful.

Please note that information about how to help children cope with loss and death is not included in this chapter, since many excellent resources already exist on the topic, including Web sites (Barrharris.org; Dougy.org; Nasponline.org) and books.[1,2,3] I do, however, provide developmental information about children's understanding of death in the following review.

Developmental Overview

I hope this synopsis of children's cognitive and emotional development provides a context for understanding your children and how to write your Final Words to them. The following information is drawn from general developmental science and my own applications. [4,5] Information about how children and adolescents understand death is also incorporated in separate age sections.

Birth to Age Seven

Learning occurs at a sensory-motor level as prelanguage experiences are stored nonverbally between **birth and age three.** It is important to emphasize that although this isn't verbal learning, it is learning nonetheless. So when little Jamell is told, "Be a big boy, don't cry," he may not understand why, but he *senses* there is something wrong with feeling the way he does, and he learns to hide his vulnerability. In comparison, little girls sense the permission for having and showing vulnerable feelings, including crying. Indeed, as a group, girls also experience more comfort when they express vulnerability, and boys experience more shame. Though neither child can put this into words now, children have emotions at this age, and they are learning lessons about what to do with them.

Developmentally speaking, **four-to-seven-year-old** children are on top of the world. Stanley Greenspan refers to this time as, *The world is my oyster!* [6] All children generally have an equal shot at being king or queen of the playground now. It's a great time of life. In terms of cognitive development, Jean Piaget's cognitive theory places these children in the later stage of preoperational thinking, which is characterized by an intu- itive style.[7] This refers to relying on sensory rather than logical information. For example, if a child watches water poured from a tall and narrow glass into a short and wide dish, the child believes there is less water in the dish, because this is what their sense of sight tells them.

As children age, their cognitive-emotional development continues. Emotions first evident in earlier years are still present, but psychological connections become more sophisti- cated. Rather than relying on a felt sense, children can use verbal language to describe their feelings as well as their rela- tionships. And although the world may be their oyster, chil- dren's own sense of power and grandeur can also frighten them. For example, little Luke is angry he has to leave his Tonka trucks to come inside for dinner. He has a meltdown because he's tired and hungry. So Luke lashes out in anger, "I wish you'd crash your car!" and stomps back outside. But once he gets there, he begins to feel scared because it *could* happen. After all, he's *king of the playground* and the *world is his oyster*. Due to this false sense of omnipotence, when writing Final Words to children younger than eight years old, it is impor- tant to clearly convey that the parent's death had nothing whatsoever to do with the child.

Children go through a series of stages in their under- standing of death. Until approximately age five, children often think of death as reversible, temporary, and impersonal.[8] This explains why young children are generally unable to show sorrow or grief in an adult way. Their understanding of death is based not only on their cognitive level, but also on what they observe around them. Watching cartoon characters rise up whole again after having been crushed does not teach children about the permanence of death. It isn't until between the ages of five and seven that most children begin to realize that death is final and that all living things die, yet at this age they still do not see death as personal, as something that will eventually happen to them. Children believe that somehow they can escape through their own trickery and masterful efforts, projecting their fear of death onto safer objects and people. At this young age children need a way to contain their fear of death, and such projection provides safe distance. The rituals with my children that I described earlier in this chapter were geared for this developmental stage, providing a familiar container for the unknown aspect of death.

Ages Eight to Eleven

New at this age is children's ability to "blend" emotions. Blending refers to mixing two different emotions together toward the same person, experience, or object. Feeling anger and love toward a parent is one example. Researchers note that the ability to blend a positive and negative feeling is first observed during this eight-to-eleven age period,[9] but I've observed that it can also occur with children as young as age five. An illustration of this is the child who is afraid of death but can blend a reassuring feeling with this scared feeling; one result is that the fear doesn't become a persistent anxiety or phobia. This blending ability is related to the development of more advanced cognitive skills. Indeed, at the beginning of puberty, the brain experiences another wave of growth that is responsive to laying down new networks in the prefrontal cortex and cerebellum, where higher reasoning is involved.[10] Children at this age no longer rely solely upon sensing and intuition. As they approach ages eleven and up, they are better able to observe and draw accurate conclusions. (They now know that water poured from the tall, thin glass into the short, wide dish is still the same amount of water.)

With more sophisticated cognitive development, it is not surprising that between the ages of eight and ten, children fully comprehend that death is irreversible. They realize that all living things die, that their parents and siblings can die, and that they, too, will die some day. A recent study showed that children between ages seven and eleven can acknowledge that physical functioning ceases at death and can provide the correct biological justifications.[11] The older children in this study also claimed that spiritual functioning continues after death and offered religious justifications for this belief. These results suggest that religious belief may serve as a protective factor at this stage. Children at every age benefit from death education, but this is the age at which children are beginning to grasp more adultlike perspectives.

Ages Twelve to Fifteen

Early to mid-adolescence sees the development of more advanced abstract reasoning abilities. These young teens are more aware of complex emotions such as feeling indignant, humiliated, frustrated, or euphoric. But keep in mind that the primary emotions of mad, scared, sad, and happy lie beneath these more complicated cognitive emotions. The ability to think abstractly also allows teens to reflect more closely on the causes of death. They are forced to begin reconciling their adolescent sense of immortality with the reality that they, and their loved ones, can and will die.[12]

It is also important to consider how social influences may affect teen's beliefs about death and their ability to cope with an actual death. Ever sensitive to the opinions of peers, traumatic deaths such as suicide, homicide, and drug overdoses can take on added meaning. If the loved one of a teen died in an atypical way, the teen may fear peer rejection or being ostracized. And when teens hide their grief or shut it down as a way to avoid social concerns, they may not receive the comfort that can help their healing process. Similarly, teens may not know how to reach out to a friend whose loved one died in a traumatic or atypical way. They will benefit from specific guidance from adults regarding how to cope with such deaths.

Ages Sixteen to Twenty-one

Parents often begin to see their children as mini-adults at this age. And in many respects, this is justified. The prefrontal cortex is more on line, but it does not complete its development until the end of puberty. And for some adolescents this can extend into the twenties. The prefrontal cortex can be called the "CEO" of the brain, because it is responsible for higher-level reasoning skills that help with complex thoughts and emotions. It analyzes and infers, and it controls attention, working memory, organization, and mood. As the prefrontal cortex matures, there is better reasoning and judgments and more control over impulses. Another part of the brain that grows through adolescence is the cerebellum, which works like a math coprocessor to improve higher thought, mathematics, music, philosophy, decision making, and interpersonal relations.[13] If all goes well, by the end of adolescence teens have the necessary tools to both feel and express their emotions, to blend, to analyze, to regulate, and to empathize. But as previously discussed, social forces such as gender roles and stereotypes can either sharpen or blunt these tools.

Since adolescents' ways of thinking about death now are more similar to those of an adult, it makes for more familiar terrain for parents. Some teens may begin developing philosophical perspectives and become intrigued with the meaning of life.[14] If they believe in God, some may question how a loving God could let their loved one die. This can lead to confusion or despair. It can also lead to the decision to disengage from loved ones in order to avoid suffering future pain and grief. The presence of ongoing death education is critical as teens become (statistically) more likely to experience the loss of friends and loved ones. In response to this, some teens may begin taking unnecessary chances with their lives in order to confront death and overcome their fears by exercising control over mortality. Such behavior mimics the magical thinking of younger children, who may believe, *If I can defy this close encounter, then somehow I am in control of the bad things in my life—like loss and death.* Another way that adolescents may react to death is to begin the process of death denial with which many adults are familiar.

Developmental Caveat

While it is helpful to know that children and teens go through a series of developmental stages in their cognitive-emotional development and in their understanding of death, it is important to remember that development occurs at individual rates. So any guideline presented should be considered as just that—a guideline rather than a specific timetable or prescription. It is equally important to keep in mind that all children experience death uniquely and have their own ways of coping based on their temperament and life experiences. Some children ask questions about death as early as three years old. Others may outwardly appear to be unconcerned about the death of a grandparent, but react strongly to the death of a pet. Some may never mention death, yet act out feelings and thoughts in their play.

Circumstances surrounding the death of a loved one can affect children's and teens' thoughts and feelings in ways we least expect. Knowing how much children understand and how much they can handle may give parents necessary information to help children navigate through cultural messages about death as well as through their own personal experiences. There isn't a clear map for this journey. However, empathetic, nonjudgmental responses from adults, along with careful listening and watching, are excellent rudders.

Transcending Fear and Death Denial: Final Words to Children

Death beliefs and teachings can be conveyed to children in ways that are consistent with any religious tradition. As shared at the beginning of this chapter, the concrete idea that my family could somehow extend into the next life seemed to satisfy my children's need at the time while also keeping unnecessary fear at bay. It is also important to note that I was able to introduce talking about death with them before they had experienced the sudden death of a friend or family member. But initial conversations and lessons can come at any time. Indeed, they are often prompted by the actual death of loved ones or pets.

We have a beautiful drawing of a divine being that is embracing a person who has just arrived in what appears to be heaven. I love this picture because it offers comfort on two levels. It not only suggests that what comes next is good, but it also comforts those who can no longer care for the loved one who died. I had hoped that sharing this with my children a couple of years ago might be another way to help them conceptualize death in a hopeful way. I got some verification of this when one of my daughters, then ten years old, was eating lunch in the school cafeteria with her classmates. For reasons unknown to me, the lunch conversation turned to what they would do if both of their parents died at the same time. One child said she would want to kill herself so she could be with her parents. Another said life would always be horrible after that. My daughter's response was rather pragmatic (and hopeful), as she pointed out, "You can't be sad forever."

By talking about death with children, parents lay the foundation for future conversations and the possibility of positive grief adjustment. The truth is that there is no way to predict how a child will respond to a sudden death or the expected loss of a loved one. But we do know that religious rituals and spiritual teachings can help children conceptualize a very abstract and unknown experience. Photographs are also helpful, especially for young children, who are intuitive and concrete in their thinking. In fact, the nature of concrete thinking explains why adults should never tell a young child that a dead person is "just sleeping." Children have developed fears of sleeping after being given this well-intended but frightening explanation.

I believe that children come naturally pointed toward hopeful and spiritual ways. Words from parents and other adults can continue helping them to head in this direction. I hope that some of this developmental information helps guide your dialogues about death and assists you in crafting a healing legacy to your children.

Important Writing Decisions

To date, I have not talked with a child who has received Final Words from a parent. My hope is that it would provide healing along their grief journey. Thus, I would be very interested in learning about how children receive Final Words and how they later reflect on them as adults. In any event, as parents prepare their final message, specific issues may arise that are related to writing to children.

What Age? What to Write?

When writing Final Words to your children, the first decision is "what age" your children will be when they read them. By this I mean that your child may be ten years old when you write, but you expect them to be reading your Final Words as an adult. The tone of this writing will likely be an "ageless" voice that transcends youth and adulthood, conveying deep and meaningful life lessons. If Final Words are written in this way, they don't necessarily need to be rewritten or updated. Another option is to write to your child with the assumption that your Final Words will be read when he or she is young. If this is the case, you will likely revise your Final Words as your child becomes a teen or adult and adapt the words, tone, and content accordingly.

Once you have decided the age your child should be when he or she reads your Final Words, the next decision is what you will say. Chapter 4 provides necessary background and specific ideas. There is also an outline of Final Words in appendix 1 that may be helpful. But there are some unique themes in the parent-child relationship that merit separate discussions.

Advice and Milestones

It is almost impossible to convey all the advice that parents want children to have in the parents' absence. However, if you want to attempt this important task, I strongly recommend doing so, because it can bring great peace of mind. I recall the story of a young mother who died of cancer. Since she was terminally ill for almost a year, she had a lot of time to leave final messages for her children. The form she chose was to videotape messages to each child on their advancing birthdays. You can imagine how each birthday message reflected developmental and social changes in the children's lives. You can also imagine what an amazing legacy this was.

We all want—perhaps expect—to be present for our children's milestones: first dates, high school and college graduations, engagement and marriage, parenthood. We also expect to be present for the sad times: first heartbreak, not making the team, not reaching an academic or career goal, illnesses, and every other curve that life throws their way. While most of us will indeed be present to advise and share with our children, there is obviously no guarantee that we will be there. So as you craft your healing legacy, you get to decide how much to say. A sixty-five-year-old woman I know addressed specific milestones when she wrote to her children and grandchildren. My current Final Words include broader messages about life rather than milestones. Our different approaches may reflect our different personalities, values, life experiences, or religious beliefs. And neither is right or wrong. We write according to who we are, and that is what makes our legacy *our* legacy.

Core Messages

One of the reasons I decided to write broad "core messages" to my children is that this is the view I gleaned when I looked back at my life from the eternity perspective. I had a sense of no longer needing to micromanage their lives. I just wanted to support them in making healthy decisions, being happy, and staying close to God. I figured that these three core messages would carry them through the good and bad parts of their lives. Other core messages that parents may wish to convey include expressions of pride, confidence, kindness, faith, family legacy, ethics, values, and specific lessons (especially lessons that the parent learned in his or her life).

Hope. Many core messages could be singled out. I focus on hope first because the death of a parent can often negatively affect a child's hope or belief that life can be joyful again. For this reason it seems important to help reinstill a hope in a parent's final message to children. It may be as simple as reminding them that time will help heal their pain, or sharing how an experience of grief eventually healed for you, especially if you lost a parent. Although grief is experienced and expressed differently among children, I encourage you to include a specific message in your Final Words that can help children hope for a return to joy.

Forgiveness. When writing Final Words to young children, parents may need to ask for forgiveness. It may be for small transgressions, or it may be for very hurtful behaviors. But the statements will be similar: "I am truly sorry for the way I hurt you when . . . I hope you can experience forgiveness." Related to this, it may be important to include a statement that your children are not at fault for any of your behaviors or decisions. Since children and adolescents are developmentally egocentric (thinking the world revolves around them), they may feel responsible for things that went wrong such as a divorce or a parents' illness or unhappiness. Given this possibility, it is important to clearly relieve children of any real or perceived burden of guilt that they may be carrying. Parents can do this by simply including an earnest statement that the child was not responsible for any of these things.

If your child or teen was clearly to blame for hurting you or negatively affecting the family, it is important to express forgiveness. Having this in writing can be a touchstone of healing that extends throughout your child's life. If you find it difficult to do this, please consider talking with someone who will support you in finding a way to forgive your child.

One Parent's Final Words

I hesitated about including an example of Final Words. I don't want to suggest that this—or any other example—is the right way. What parents choose to write to their children is a very unique and intimate experience. Any of the information presented in this book is intended to serve as a guide or suggestions. With this caveat, I provide an excerpt of Final Words that a friend graciously agreed to share:

Dear David,

I am writing this to you when I am 44 years old and in good health. You are eleven and also healthy. There are so many things I want to say to you. Let me begin by telling you how much I love you and I could not have asked for a better son. Your kindness and sense of humor have been such a gift to me . . . ever since you were a toddler! I am proud of how well you do in school, and especially so because reading has been hard for you. I remember how spelling eventually got easier for me, but it was really hard in elementary school. I admire how you go to school every day and face this challenge. I think you have much courage.

Please know that though I won't be here on earth as you go through the rest of your life, if I can, I will watch over you. And if you carry my love in your heart, I am always with you. Many wonderful parts of life await you and I want you to enjoy all of those . . . friends, basketball season, college, falling in love, making your own home. There will be disappointments as well. Your courageous spirit will take you through all of those. As you know, there is a courageous spirit in the face of challenges in my family, and I am glad you are there to carry on this legacy.

You may feel so sad and angry about my death. That's okay and normal. Please be sure to get comfort from your dad and Carin [older sister] and Uncle Rod and Aunt Sarah. Talk to them or cry with them. Please know that someday you will feel happy and better . . . it took me a while to feel better after my mother died, but I did. And you will, too.

Love,

Your Mom

Writing Legacy Letters to Young Children

When the course of life goes as we expect and hope it will, children do not die before their parents. But if a parent is faced with this ultimate loss and wants to write a final legacy letter of affirmation and good-bye, then I hope something in this book is helpful. I defer to grief experts, hospice workers, and medical professionals to provide specific resources for parents of terminally ill children. Talking about a child's death as well as how to leave nothing unsaid is both delicate and important. There is growing research in this area, including a recent study involving 449 parents who lost children to cancer. None of the parents who had talked with the children about the child's impending death regretted having such a discussion. However, nearly one-third of the parents who didn't have such conversations now regret that choice.[15]

The focus now turns to writing Legacy Letters of celebration to mark milestones in the lives of children and teens. Many of us have given notes of love or gratitude to our children. While such notes and poems are valuable in their own right, they differ from Legacy Letters. As discussed in chapter 5, these letters can be written to mark an important occasion and to convey specific messages. As I talked with parents who have written this type of celebratory letter to their children, I learned that these letters often echo an eternal perspective, not unlike Final Words. So as you craft your letter, please keep in mind that your words may ultimately serve in this way for your young or adult children. Below I share the experiences of two different families who have written Legacy Letters of celebration to their children over the years.

Ben is a middle-aged father of two children, ages twenty-one and seventeen. He runs a successful business in financial advising. Ben describes himself as logical, organized, and competitive. When asked if he thought of himself as emotional, he chuckled and said that neither he nor anyone else would describe him that way. So it was surprising that he eagerly described the intimate letters he had written to his children when they turned thirteen. The idea came to him as he watched his parents aging. He realized that they would not be there forever for him, and that he in turn would not always be there for his own children. Ben's decision to write was therefore more logical than emotional. When his children became teenagers, he wanted to give them advice and guidance. He also wanted them to know how much they were loved and that they could always come to him, no matter what. Ben described how the letters had a similar purpose in this way. But since the children were very different from each other, the content of the letters also reflected these differences.

Ben's children received their letters with what he called "quiet gratitude." They did not cry or tell him it was the best thing in the world. They simply read the letters, thanked him, and put them in a special place for safekeeping. Ben later decided he would write letters again when they turned eighteen. At the time of our conversation, he had given his eldest child the letter and was beginning to formulate what he would say to his next high school graduate. Ben chuckled again at how different his children have turned out and that this next letter would *definitely* be a different kind of letter.

Christine is a mother of three and works full time as a nurse. What's different about her letters of celebration is that she wrote them jointly with her husband. Christine organized the ritual, and Steve, her husband, willingly participated. They wrote letters to their children before each went off to college. Like Ben, Christine and Steve found themselves writing similar themes of advice, family legacy, and values to all three children. But each letter ended up being different from the others, because the children were all so different from one another. Christine and Ben talked openly about this tradition, so each child came to expect—and look forward to—"the letter" the summer before going to college.

Stated previously, Legacy Letters is a name I have given to such letters, since they are a type of legacy. Referring to these important messages as simply "the letter" is likely all that is needed for family members who have started this tradition. It matters less what we call them as long as they are written.

Writing Final Words and Legacy Letters to Adult Children

As parents reflect on the adult lives of their children, it is important to know that cognitive, emotional, and social development continue through adulthood. A significant body of research about this exists within developmental psychology. An accessible chronology of social-emotional lifespan development can be found by looking at adult life transitions. Though dated now, Gail Sheehy's bestseller *Passages* outlined many normative transitions from the "trying twenties" to the "fabulous fifties" and beyond.[16] These include, but are not limited to, starting a career, partnering or marrying, raising a family, succeeding in jobs/careers, and retiring. These milestones—or passages—are expected in mainstream culture.

But what if your son or daughter does not achieve some or all of these transitions? This is an aspect of your child's adult development that you may wish to address in Final Words and Legacy Letters. Why? Two salient features of the adult child-parent relationship include whether children know their parents are proud of them and whether parents see their children as being "a good son" or "a good daughter." So as you write final messages to your adult children, I encourage you to speak to these issues. Discussed earlier in the book, shadows can blur what is real or needed. Layers of shame or depression about not measuring up to societal—or parental—expectations can be washed away by a parent's blessing or affirmation. Similarly, the loneliness and grief associated with not marrying or having children, or losing one's job and not achieving career goals, can be comforted by parents' words of pride and support. The reasons that adult children may not enjoy all the traditional life passages may include illness, poverty, discrimination, or legal issues. One example that comes to mind is how gay or lesbian young adults may encounter roadblocks that keep them from getting married. In the end, the reasons matter less than how the adult child and his or her family respond. I hope that this awareness provides some perspective and empathy for adult children who may not smoothly pass through predictable life transitions.

Adult children who are successful by society's standards also need to hear the same messages of pride and affirmation. Parental validation that a child has been a good son or daughter is a universal elixir. And since no one escapes pain or disappointment in life, conveying support and comfort for life's expected difficulties (past, present, or future) is important to share with adult children who have, thus far, succeeded in their life goals and adjusted to normative transitions.

It can be very challenging to write Final Words and Legacy Letters to adult children who are estranged or with whom there is a history of conflict. Some of the suggestions in this book can help guide your words and writing. If you get stuck in disappointment, bitterness, or resentment, or just simply can't find your way out of the conflict, many resources exist to help you move forward in order to create a healing legacy. Shadow work, journaling, and talking with a trusted other who can both support and confront you are some examples. Friends, family, mentors, clergy, spiritual directors, and therapists can be valuable in this reflection process.

When writing Final Words and Legacy Letters, it is important for parents to keep in mind that adult children need to know, just as much as younger children do, that they are forgiven for how they may have intentionally or unintentionally hurt their parents. Some adults may also still need reassurance that they were not the cause of their parent's unhappiness, illness, or misfortune (financially or otherwise). And if for some reason they were, then they need to know they are forgiven. As described in previous discussions of forgiveness, if you have difficulty forgiving your son or daughter, please consider talking with someone who can help you work through this important issue.

When discussing the idea of Final Words with my friend Rob, he asked if it would be appropriate to tell an adult child it was time to "grow up." I discuss this question in the next chapter. For now, I simply want to acknowledge the difference between healthy shame (you have *done something* bad) and toxic shame (you *are* bad). There is a place for healthy shame in everyone's lives. But toxic shame is the stuff that chronic depression and misery are made of. If you are in doubt about how a "just grow up" message might sound, get feedback by talking about it with someone else, or ask an objective person to read it.

Explaining Final Words

After reading about the idea of Final Words or after writing them, some parents may introduce their younger children to death by telling them about the special letter they will receive when the parent dies. Children may ask to read the letter now rather than later. You can handle this as you wish, but I recommend keeping your Final Words for after your death and writing a Legacy Letter of celebration for your children to read now.

Upon learning about the idea of final messages, it is also possible that children or teens will want to write Final Words to their loved ones. When we flew overseas not too long ago, one of my daughters left a letter with a final message for a close friend—just in case. If your children decide they want to write Final Words, I have created sample outlines for children and teens to follow in the appendix section. Although children sometimes need structure or suggestions to get going, invite them to try to write independently before reading the outline to allow freedom and creativity to be their guides.

There are many ways children learn about death from their parents. This may include role modeling and experiencing the death of a loved one together. Other ways children learn with their parents' guidance might be through bibliography (books that directly teach or tell a metaphorical story), religious teachings from respective denominations, and simple conversations about death. Such conversations can happen whenever the topic comes up. Children are curious and want to know about everything. Most parents have discovered that very important conversations can even happen while driving back and forth from school, soccer, or swim team.

Keep in mind that since death is so hidden in developed countries, parents may need to initiate the conversations. Indeed, whenever I have simply asked my children if they had any questions about death, they always did. Telling your younger children or adult children about your Final Words will likely invite reflection about your relationship and hopefully encourage further discussions about death—and life.

For Grandparents

Many parents who are reading this chapter may also be (or will eventually be) grandparents. If this is the case and you wish to leave final messages to your grandchildren, please do. You will need to decide whether to write individual letters or to write a group letter. Only you will know which best fits your legacy to them. Many of the themes and ideas in this chapter may also apply to grandparents. If not in specific ways, then perhaps the themes and ideas can provide a general context for your reflections. And perhaps some of the developmental information will be helpful as you craft a legacy to this future progeny.

Summary for Parents

This chapter acknowledges unique aspects of the parent-child relationship that can be reflected in the themes of Final Words and Legacy Letters. It also suggests that discussing Final Words with children, teens, and adult children may serve as a type of death education or conversation starter. The tone of parents' Final Words will vary according to children's ages and their cognitive and emotional development. Or perhaps parents will write final messages using an ageless voice that transcends time and includes core themes that reach across the lifespan. Legacy Letters of celebration and affirmation written to young children, teens, and adult children are a wonderful way to communicate—and commemorate—certain milestones. Though not intended to be last messages, such letters can also serve as Final Words. Regardless of the form, ensuring that the written word honors the relationship between parent and child in some way is the essence of a healing legacy.

✺ CHAPTER 9 ✺

A DIFFERENT KIND OF
INHERITANCE

MR. FLOWERS WAS a good and generous man who was loved by our community. While I was writing this book, he was diagnosed with terminal cancer. My husband, John, was especially fond of Mr. Flowers because of the help he had extended to John back in college. John was one of countless people who visited Mr. Flowers at the end of his life to reminisce and say good-bye in their own way. During one visit, John expressed appreciation again to Mr. Flowers for his help and went on to describe the positive effect it had on his life. Mr. Flowers glowed when he learned that his gift had made such a difference. So John's good-bye was bittersweet. He was sad as he listened to Mr. Flowers talk about preparing for death, but he also felt grateful to know he had returned a gift in kind.

On what everyone knew would be Mr. Flowers's last birthday, a neighbor organized a community birthday celebration. People met at a nearby corner and walked down the street, in parade fashion, to his house. Mr. Flowers's daughter led him to the door at the designated time as more than a hundred people gathered in front of the house with a large banner. I have never heard a more meaningful rendition of the "Happy Birthday" song.

You can imagine how touched Mr. Flowers was by this act of generosity. As people began forming a reception line to speak personally with him, I noticed a small, brown wicker basket sitting on the front lawn. Blue and gold Mylar balloons, floating above, were tethered to the handle of the basket. It was filled to the brim with notes and cards. I don't know what people wrote to Mr. Flowers, but I assume the notes were filled with affirmations of his life.

Looking at Mr. Flowers's basket of birthday messages reminded me of my father's treasured cache of greeting cards. I thought about how important words must have been to my dad, how important they are to all of us. It seems fitting that we would exchange words, something that becomes a part of us, at the end of a life.

There is another central part to this story. During his last months, Mr. Flowers wrote a letter to his loved ones. He called it "A Message of Thanks" and requested that it be read at his funeral. The letter began with "Dear Family and Friends" and went on to express his genuine appreciation to all the people in his life. Some were mentioned by name; others were included in a general blessing that acknowledged how each person attending the funeral had helped him in some way, even if they did not know how. Mr. Flowers also thanked everyone for the notes and cards given to him during the end of his life; he said they meant more to him than we could ever know. Those of us who had the privilege of listening to his final message received closure in a way that is difficult to describe. *We heard Mr. Flowers's final words.* While we were so sad that he was gone, his words lifted us in a transcending and real way. And it was all because this good man made the difficult but generous decision to write personal words of farewell to be read after he died—a different kind of inheritance, indeed.

This story is included here to show how writing final messages can be meaningful to both the writer and receiver. But even more than that, it suggests that perhaps some thoughts and feelings are best expressed—and preserved—by the written word.

Questions and Answers about Writing Final Words and Legacy Letters

Maggie Callanan and Patricia Kelly are experienced hospice nurses who have conducted research on dying people and the behaviors they exhibit. Their research reveals how the dying are always communicating to us about what is happening in their dying process. Working in that sacred space between life and death, these hospice nurses offer lessons worth remembering:

> Most people, when they're dying, want to feel that their having been alive has been significant, that they made some difference

in this world and in the lives of those around them. For all of us, some periodic review of how our lives are going, and recognition of our achievements, may help us find more enjoyment and purpose in our lives. At the same time some recognition of our unfinished business or troubled relationships may lead us to try and to heal some problem areas now, rather than waiting until we are dying. This could enrich our lives and prevent frantic attempts at reconciliation when it is almost too late.[1]

As observed in Mr. Flowers's final letter to his loved ones and in our last notes to him, writing final messages allows us to affirm one another, complete unfinished business, and die peacefully. And if we write such legacies when we are well, as Callanan and Kelly suggest, our current lives can be enriched.

As you consider creating a healing legacy, you still may have unanswered questions or concerns. Some may be specific to your life situation, specific relationships, or your personality. Others may be more universal. After reading the previous chapters, you may also have minor quibbles or major doubts about creating this new ritual. To address the wide range of issues that may still be present for readers, I begin this final chapter with a series of questions and answers. The questions were generated by people who shared their thoughts and feedback about writing Final Words and Legacy Letters with me over the past couple of years.

What if I really don't like a family member or significant other?

There is no legal or cultural mandate for anyone to write Final Words or Legacy Letters, so if for some reason you don't like a significant other, you are free not to write such letters. But if you decide you still want to, there are basically two ways to proceed. One is to state the truth in a nonjudgmental way. This could involve acknowledging how the relationship wasn't close and that the two of you never really got to know the other. You could offer an explanation. Or if there is none, simply let the acknowledgment stand on its own. If you have regrets about this or wish the relationship could have been better, it would be appropriate to express those feelings. Most of us know people with whom we don't "click." Or we have relationships where there is some kind of tension. This is a normal part of life. If you decide that the relationship is something that cannot improve or be resolved, you can still express good wishes for this person.

Since I believe people give and receive healing, and that this may be facilitated through Final Words and Legacy Letters, most of my responses in this question and answer section address ways to improve relationships or move beyond interpersonal conflict. Thus, another way to proceed if you really don't like someone is to reexamine the conflict, especially if there is a small voice inside that is nudging you to make the situation better. When you strongly dislike a significant person in your life, it may be helpful to explore whether it is caused by resentment. If so, address that emotion before deciding to write—or not to write. When you dislike someone, it can be a result of how that person has hurt you or someone you love. Stated another way, it is very rare to simply "dislike" your parents, wife, father, sister, or child. The relationship usually becomes toxic *because something happened*. So while we may not like a loved one's personality, at some level we love them. Let this become your compass.

If you discover that your dislike is related to bitterness or resentment, Final Words or Legacy Letters may be an opportunity for forgiveness and healing—for you. It is always wonderful when the forgiveness can occur in relationship with the other person (i.e., one apologizes and the other forgives). But this is not necessary to experience forgiveness; it is possible to forgive someone even if they don't apologize or take responsibility for their actions. This doesn't mean that you must let them come back into your life or home. It just means letting go of the anger, resentment, and "dislike" you are holding on to. It means healing emotionally. And when you are healed, the Legacy Letter or Final Words you chose to write to this person can naturally follow. As with most things in life, if you work on this alone and don't make progress, seek support from a friend, clergy, or professional helper.

My final response to this question is the story of a dying elderly mother, Emily, and her adult daughter, Elsie. Their relationship was conflicted and had brought much emotional pain to Elsie's life. When Elsie was visiting on what would likely be the last time they would ever see each other, she had no idea what to say. And yet, despite the tremendous burden that Emily had created in Elsie's life, she still loved her mother at some level. Indeed it is natural to feel both anger and love toward parents who have hurt us. But when it happens for a very long time, and we no longer feel attached or experience positive interactions, we can lose sight of love that is still there.

Words of love had never been exchanged between Elsie and her mother. But during this visit, Elsie made a courageous decision to tell her mother that she loved her. After Elsie said, "I love you, Ma. It's too bad we fought for so long," Emily's reply was shocking. As if it were the most natural response in the world, she said, "But that's what mothers and daughters do. And I love you, too." They hugged and cried and tried to figure out why they had fought for so long. The explanation that Elsie pieced together was that Emily gave what she could, what she had. Emily's mother had died when she was six months old and her father was a cruel man. Not surprisingly, Emily parented Elsie with the same disdain and absence of nurturing that had been bequeathed to her. So it was not that Emily *didn't* give Elsie what she needed; perhaps Emily *couldn't*. Realizing this made all the difference in the world to Elsie.

This true story is not meant to imply that a lifetime load is lifted in one exchange. But it does remind us that openings occur when we least expect them, especially if we are brave enough to create the opening. It is also true that many relationships may not end with a moment of reconciliation or healing in this life. Yet as Emily and Elsie's story reveals, despite decades of disdain, love doesn't necessarily die.

How do you get someone to look past dislike or make amends with someone to write Final Words and Legacy Letters?

You cannot make someone forgive another person. You can, however, give them a reason to make amends or work on forgiveness. One way to do this is to tell a meaningful story about forgiveness in your life, or share how you came to forgive someone in order to create a healing legacy. There are many other ways you can try to get someone to do the right thing. But the bottom line is that you cannot *make* someone write Final Words or Legacy Letters, because it is ultimately their decision.

How can you guarantee that manipulative and guilt-provoking people will rise above such tendencies and write honest Final Words and Legacy Letters?

Most people are not "all bad" or "all good." People can make mistakes and people can improve themselves. It is important to keep this in mind when considering an individual's manipulative or guilt-provoking behaviors. There are many causes of manipulation, but they generally fall into two categories of behavior: antisocial and adaptive.

It is believed a person with an antisocial personality disorder (formerly referred to as "sociopathy") does not have a conscience and does not feel remorse for hurting others; rather, others are viewed as objects of gratification. Manipulative behavior is merely a means toward an end, and it does not matter how those ends are achieved. People who manipulate relationships through lying and other forms of self-aggrandizement have also been referred to as evil or narcissistic. When manipulative and guilt-provoking behaviors are a function of adaptation, it is believed that such a person has learned these behaviors as an unconscious defensive posture to manage their vulnerability.

My response to the question refers mostly to people who are manipulative through adaptation rather than as a result of an antisocial personality disorder (which theoretically cannot change). Usually when people realize that someone is being manipulative or guilt provoking as a way to control the relationship, they stop socializing or withdraw from this person. But when that person is a parent, sibling, child, or other close relative, doing so may be difficult. Some may avoid the person as much as possible; others may learn to set firm boundaries and put a permanent hold on trust. All of these responses are legitimate, since no one wants to be used or made to feel guilty. But the problem with avoiding a person who is manipulative or guilt provoking is that the person never gets the necessary feedback to change his or her behaviors. So if a person who uses manipulation to control the relationships in their lives asks you for feedback about their Final Words or Legacy Letters, I hope you will be very direct and honest. Help them edit away the guilt, and if it seems right, confront them with their manipulation.

It is just as likely that a manipulative person may write and never ask for feedback. But this doesn't mean that the receiver must be subjected to more hurtful behavior from this person. The receiver is actually in a very powerful position. One option is to choose not to read anything from this person. Another is to ask a trusted friend or family member to read it first to conduct an "emotional safety check." We can hope that when looking into eternity, people will do the right thing. But we can't always count on it. So proceed with caution.

When there has been an ongoing family conflict in which sides were chosen, how do you handle this when writing Final Words or Legacy Letters?

When sides are chosen in a family conflict, there is an assumption that it is impossible to "play Switzerland" and remain neutral. Yet I have seen people successfully take neutral and diplomatic positions in families, work settings, and friendships. This diplomacy is based in a simple and logical truth: you cannot carry another person's resentment, grudge, or battle. Why not? Because it's *theirs*.

So if you haven't been able to overtly state your love, concern, or care for all people involved in the conflict, this would be a time to do so. On the one hand, you are modeling healthy and noble behavior. On the other, you also run the risk of offending someone who may have been hurt by the very person(s) for whom you express magnanimous views. If you worry about offending someone, go ahead and express this concern in your writing. At the core of most conflicts, even the person who is hurt most knows that taking the high road is the way to go.

How can you guarantee that someone will be "real" in their Final Words and not be politically correct or create a false legacy and contrived feelings?

You can probably guess the answer to this question. There is no way that anyone can guarantee a person will do the right thing. Perhaps one way to think about this particular issue is to shift the focus from the writer to the reader. Though the writer has the power of words, the reader has the power of discernment—to decide what is true and read between the lines. Similar to the situation in which the writer might be manipulative, the reader also always has the power to decide if, when, and how to read the Final Words and Legacy Letters that they receive.

When writing Final Words, is it okay to tell someone to "get their act together"?

If you remain concerned that a loved one is headed down the wrong path or has stayed on that wrong path for too long, you can use your Final Words to convey this. But I encourage you to carefully choose your words. The phrase "get your act together" has a shaming tone. Direct but kinder feedback is recommended. For example, if a sibling has a substance abuse problem and you have previously expressed this to that person, you could write, "As you know, I have been concerned about your marijuana use over the years. I hope you can find a way to stop using. I wish I could have helped you more. The decision to stop must begin with you. But support is there, in many ways, when you ask. Please do. I know you can do it."

Although this example focuses on substance abuse, it could also refer to someone's philandering behavior, irresponsible spending, or untreated physical or mental illness. When you are direct but kind, your words have a greater chance of being heard. If you have not previously talked with this person about your concern, you can still be direct and kind in your writing and perhaps explain what prevented you from talking directly with them about it in the past.

If you are in doubt about how to word this issue in your

final messages, it might be wise to ask a person who can be objective to read your Final Words and see how the "get your act together" message comes across. If after taking these steps you are still unsure, it may be best to refrain from addressing these concerns in your final messages.

How do you address sibling rivalry/conflict in final messages?

When a parent writes Final Words to their children, one of the first decisions is whether to write a group letter or to write separate letters to individual children. How you address sibling rivalry or any sibling conflict will vary depending on which format you choose. A general way to address these issues is to name your awareness of it and, if it applies, apologize for your role in ignoring or creating it. If you have been wrongly accused of favoring one child over another, you can simply state that you have been misunderstood and set the record straight. It will also help to state how you love each child equally and how if you showed this in different ways, it was not intentional. And if it is important to you that any lingering sibling conflicts be resolved, such wishes can be very powerful when expressed in final messages.

If an adult child writes Final Words or a Legacy Letter to a parent when there has been a history of rivalry or conflict between siblings that created distress, at least two decisions must be made. Will you address it? And if so, why—what is the purpose or desired outcome? If it is to convey guilt or resentment, then that does not belong in a healing legacy. But if it is to convey awareness and forgiveness, then please do so.

When siblings have been unsuccessful at resolving conflicts

or initiating reconciliation with their sibling(s) while still living, then writing a Legacy Letter or Final Words can be one way to heal some of those wounds.

What if I needed or wanted Final Words from someone and didn't get them?

I recall a story about a middle-aged man whose father was dying of cancer. Their relationship was filled with conflict throughout their lives. The father, Mr. Ruiz, held on to his emotions and rarely displayed outward affection. The son, Mike, was the same way until he got married and became a father. Unlike his father, Mike lived in a time when men's roles had broadened and he was freer to allow his family to pull him away from the world of stoic masculinity into a world of fun, disappointment, and lots of hugs—the real world. So as Mr. Ruiz's final weeks became apparent, Mike spent a lot of time with him, hoping they might have a meaningful conversation about death, life, or love. Though this conversation wasn't happening, Mike didn't give up hope. This hope seemed rewarded when, during Mr. Ruiz's last month, Mike's mother said that his father had been spending time writing. Mike hoped his father was expressing in writing what he could not express in person. But neither happened. Mike and his father never had that conversation, and no one in Mike's family ever received or found any letters.

This is a sad outcome on many levels. It was heartbreaking for Mike to yearn his whole life to have an intimate conversation with his father and then to be further let down when he expected to receive a letter from his father and didn't. But the sadness doesn't stop there. I find myself thinking about Mr. Ruiz and how he likely lived life within the confines of an emotional straitjacket right up until he died. I find myself wondering how terribly difficult it must have been for him to try to write. I think about how sad it is that, for whatever reason, Mike's father eventually decided he couldn't share what he wrote.

I tell this story to expose the different layers of how and why people may not write final messages of good-bye. To say that it's just too hard doesn't capture the struggle that many people, especially men, may experience with emotional expression. So my answer to this question is that if a person you love did not leave you a written healing legacy, it may not be because they didn't want to. It may be that they started writing and couldn't find the right words. It might be that they died before they could finish. It could also be that they intended to write but simply got too busy with the daily demands of life, or a crisis interrupted the writing process.

For reasons you may never know, they did not write. You must consider that these reasons probably have nothing to do with you and likely have everything to do with them. But still it is sad. And while there is nothing you can do to get a healing legacy from that person, you can make sure those you love receive one.

What if I receive Final Words or a Legacy Letter that has a message I don't like or understand?

When I discussed this book with a group of people, one of them recalled the only final words that her friend Crystal received from her mother, "Always watch out for number one." Like many words, a broader context is needed to understand this mother's message. Crystal's mother had a horribly abusive childhood that later resulted in her experiencing serious mental illness as an adult. All of this limited the ability to parent effectively. Most children are not able to empathize with this perspective until they are adults, or until they have had other experiences and people that could nurture them in the way their parent could not. Viewed from this perspective, the mother's message was simply what she knew. It was *her* sage advice and legacy. Though it wasn't what Crystal wanted to hear, it was all this mother had to give.

Sometimes parents may not provide any type of final messages, or the message they give is much less than what we need. I hope this true example helps you develop an empathetic perspective for the confusing or unhelpful messages you may receive.

What if I feel too resentful to write or read Final Words or a Legacy Letter?

If you have strong feelings of resentment that you cannot resolve and still want to write to this person, you could simply acknowledge those feelings. You could go on to express any regrets about the situation as well as any positive wishes or lessons learned. If you have a desire to work through the resentment, it may be helpful to talk with a friend, professional helper, or spiritual mentor who can be objective. Such reflective conversations can help shift energy to start things changing. Indeed, when there is a logjam in a river, only one or two logs are pulled out and the current takes care of the rest. If you still feel resentful after a lot of hard work, but realize that you also love this person, perhaps a statement of love is all that needs to be expressed.

If nothing helps and you still cannot write a final message to this person, perhaps your loved ones will understand that it was too difficult. And though they may have wished for words of reconciliation, they will likely respect your struggle and know that you did the best you could.

While writing your Final Words has a sense of urgency, since you are the only one who can write them to your loved ones, *reading* someone else's Final Words is different. So if you feel resentful toward someone who wrote Final Words to you, there is a lot of time to prepare for reading them and to work through resentment. In other words, you could read them the same day you receive them—or ten years later.

What if I really don't care about leaving a healing legacy?

Whenever someone tells me that they "don't care" about something, I wonder, *Why not?* I have come to observe over time that people may decide not to care because at one time they did care very much (about someone or something) and were hurt. Not caring can be a stalwart psychological defense to protect the inner self. I have great respect for such defenses, because they develop for good reason and are designed to protect. But like any wall, as they provide shelter from harm, they can also keep goodness—and healing—from entering.

As described in this book, writing a healing legacy to loved ones can be as good for the writer as it may be for the receiver.

So regardless of the reason that you may not care about creating a healing legacy, it is important to look beyond your wants and needs. Think about the values and needs of your loved ones. They likely care very much and need final messages from you.

What if I abandoned my family? What if my parents abandoned me?

Parents can hurt their children in awful and tragic ways. Abandonment and neglect are two ways; abuse is another. I have provided counseling to the parents and the children in both of these painful circumstances. Though nothing can erase the memory of pain, healing is possible—and there are many different paths to healing.

I recently became aware of a father who abandoned his wife and four children. Back when the cultural mandate was for mothers to stay at home and care for their children, this young mother went to work full-time in order to support the family. Decades after abandoning them, the father contacted his adult children to make amends. They did not want to have any contact with him and several years later he died. The father did not leave any written correspondence to the family, perhaps out of respect for the boundary they set when they refused to reestablish communication.

This is not a story about what people should or shouldn't have done; I trust that everyone in this family did the best they could. No one ever wants to abandon his or her family, and no one ever wants to leave an open wound in their heart. But in the spirit of healing legacies, I will always wonder what would have happened if the father had written Final Words that stated something like this:

Dear Children,

It was wrong for me to abandon the family. I understand you did not want to talk with me in the past few years, and I respect this. But there are two things you need to know. First, you did nothing to make me leave; it wasn't your fault. I was weak and lost and addicted to alcohol, and I have regretted that decision every day of my life. Second, I do not ask for your forgiveness, but I do want you to know that when I left, I thought your lives would be better off without me. If I thought I could have been a good father to you, I would have stayed. You have every right to be angry with me, but please know that you did nothing wrong and that I am sorry for all the hurt and pain I caused you.

It isn't difficult to imagine how an abandoned child, whether fifteen or fifty years old, may not want to read Final Words from the parent who abandoned them. But I can't help wondering if it might have helped facilitate the healing of these children. Such a letter could fill in the blanks that they filled in themselves as a result of not having any information from or about their father. And at the very least, they might learn that their father wasn't a monster but rather a tortured human being who, though it was not nearly good enough, did the best he could. That would seem to be a very different kind of legacy than the one this family inherited.

What if I hurt my family—should I write Final Words or Legacy Letters?

We all hurt people in our families. Sometimes it is in sad and awful ways like the preceding story of abandonment. It could also be through marital infidelity or domestic violence. Sometimes the hurt is by accident, such as an unintended consequence of a selfish or foolish act. I think of two families as I write this—one that was devastated when their adult son went to prison for dealing drugs, another that was overcome with shock when their adult daughter killed a family while driving under the influence. Neither of these people set out to hurt their families. But they did.

Whether you have intentionally or unintentionally hurt someone, the only way to help them (and yourself) to heal is by taking responsibility for your actions, sincerely apologizing, and hoping for forgiveness. So I would encourage you to do all of these as you write Legacy Letters or Final Words. Legacy Letters allow for the possibility of healing a relationship while everyone is still alive. But if for some reason this is not possible, then your Final Words can create the healing legacy you were unable to begin earlier.

What if a loved one has stopped talking with me—should I still write Final Words or a Legacy Letter?

If you can determine why the person has stopped speaking, then you will know better how to proceed. But if you cannot determine why, I suggest that you do what feels most true to you. I always advocate for writing Final Words or a Legacy Letter because of the possibility for healing. But there may be situations where writing such letters is not the best course to take, and I trust that you will know if this is the case for you.

Most people want to make amends before they die, but that seems to be our trouble. We wait far too long. Writing a Legacy Letter of reconciliation while both writer and reader are still alive might be more beneficial in this situation.

I like the idea of final messages, but want to call them by a different name. Is that okay?

My mother calls her final messages "Just In Case." This title reflects the theme of her narrative, which is, *just in case you didn't know* . . . I love this name and the creative energy she put into it. But more important, my mother is pleased with it. She keeps the document with her other important papers and says that we can read it now or when she's gone (so it's a cross between Final Words and Legacy Letters). Thus, my answer to this question is, yes, of course! Call your final messages whatever you would like. And please see the next section for other creative ideas.

Other Types of Healing Legacies

While writing this book, I described the topic to Meg, a fellow swim team parent, who had recently recovered from cancer. She liked the idea of Final Words and went on to describe a similar idea she developed. She has been writing journals to her three sons since they were born. The family even has a ritual of sitting in bed on Mother's Day as Meg reads these journals out loud. They laugh together at some of the funny stories and cry together at the touching ones. During the time Meg was undergoing cancer treatment, she continued to write in her sons' journals. But the writing took on a whole different meaning. She was very aware of how, in her absence, the words might become legacies rather than memory books. This made her writing—and the very words themselves—take on a different weight and tone. As she described this I was reminded of how I felt the first time I wrote Final Words to my family. There is such gravity in finality.

Meg also reflected on how helpful it was *for her* to write. She remarked that after her brush with death, she would much prefer to die of a terminal illness (far into the future, of course) than to die from a sudden death. Meg reported feeling a sense of peace and comfort knowing that her words could provide a healing legacy to help her sons transcend their pain. And all she did was write thoughts and feelings to loved ones. Perhaps Meg's idea could be called *Legacy Journals*. I think this story provides a glimpse of what it is like to have time to prepare for final good-byes—time that all of us really have.

Renewed interest in the hobby of scrapbooks calls attention to another possible medium for creating a healing legacy. While scrapbooks have been around for a long time, the contemporary version is very detailed, with themes, colors, textures, and, of course, lots of captions and photos. While I was working with a grieving adult daughter in counseling, she reported that the scrapbooks her mother had made for her provided much comfort, especially during the first year after her mother's death. The detailed captions and thoughtfully chosen photographs were a legacy of love that truly honored their relationship. Such scrapbooks could be created for any loved one—for grandchildren, spouses, parents, and friends.

In keeping with the constantly changing revolution of technology, "electronic scrapbooks" that are digitally preserved or
saved on videotape provide another option. Many forms of
media can communicate and preserve legacies to loved ones.
When rock singer Neil Young learned that he had a potentially
fatal brain aneurysm, in the few days prior to undergoing
brain surgery he cut a new CD *(Prairie Wind)* that included
many of his final messages. He expressed intimate thoughts
and feelings as he faced—and perhaps transcended—the
meaning of life and death.[2] Though most of us don't have his
gifted musical talent, this illustrates how it is possible to use
music and other art forms to leave healing legacies.

To be sure, there are numerous types of healing legacies that
can comfort loved ones after death, and the more, the better.
We need to be talking about them and sharing them with one
another. Anytime we talk about our mortality, death becomes
less foreign and life can become more meaningful.

Forgiveness in Healing Legacies

Forgiveness has been mentioned throughout this book as an
essential element of final messages because of its healing
nature. One could also argue that forgiveness plays an important role in many other types of healing.[3, 4] Yet forgiveness can
get blocked. It is difficult to forgive when we have been
betrayed or hurt. And it is difficult to forgive when the other
person continues the hurtful behavior.

Religious leaders from every denomination have taught for
centuries that forgiveness frees both the perpetrator and the
victim. Part of this freedom involves letting go of negative

binding energy. I could be first in line to give ample reasons why it feels impossible to forgive someone who has hurt, betrayed, or traumatized you. But experience has taught me that forgiveness may be the purest form of healing. I have also learned that forgiveness is an ongoing process. Perhaps this is what Mother Teresa attempts to convey in her words, "We must make our homes centers of compassion and forgive *endlessly* [italics added]." (5)

Even with wonderful meditations to guide us, forgiveness can still be troublesome. I participated in a class where the topic of forgiveness was being discussed. A social worker, who worked with victims of domestic violence and sexual abuse, disagreed that forgiveness was necessary. She held her ground that survivors of domestic violence should not forgive their perpetrators. We all listened and understood. Withholding forgiveness is a formidable defense and means of protection. But we could also see how this woman's own resentment and anger were preventing her from seeing the fuller—and more healing—picture. Survivors of abuse can forgive but still maintain boundaries. Forgiveness does not mean forgetting or recommitting to a relationship, especially if physical safety is in question. Rather, the forgiveness being discussed in class was for the *survivor's heart* and for *her own healing*. But all of this is difficult for someone to see when they are in great pain, if they are physically unsafe, if they have never known a safe and loving relationship, or if they have never been forgiven themselves.

When we reflect on regrets about things we did or did not do in our lives as we write final messages, the regrets that involve people can often be traced to a lack of forgiveness. Either we did not forgive someone or we were not forgiven. Although I still have to work hard sometimes at simply just *wanting* to forgive, I know that forgiveness is truly best for all. I suspect you know this, too.

Throughout life we can hurt and betray others, and others can hurt and betray us. The resentment and lack of forgiveness that stems from this hurt can cause ongoing pain and suffering to individuals, families, generations—even countries. Asking for and granting forgiveness through final messages is one of the many ways that healing can happen. The last will and testament is not structured to convey forgiveness, regrets, or any type of personal communication. But we can express these thoughts and feelings—and much more—in Final Words and Legacy Letters.

Final Thoughts on Final Messages

Sometimes the letters that we write to our loved ones unintentionally become our Final Words. This happened to me after my father's sudden death. It has no doubt occurred in the lives of countless others. A recent story about Major Chris Phelps, an American fighting in the Iraq war, describes how he was exchanging good-byes with his family before deployment when he said he forgot something and went back into the house. There, he left a letter to his family on the kitchen table.[6] These messages may eventually become his Final Words, but currently they serve as a type of legacy letter to his family.

Major Phelps's decision to write that letter reflects a human desire, from deep within, to leave nothing unsaid. We can also look to art (perhaps imitating life) for another example. In John Coetzee's novel *Age of Iron,* the central character is Mrs. Curren, an older woman who is dying of cancer in apartheid South Africa.[7] As she reflects on the meaning of life and death, she is compelled to write her last thoughts and feelings to her daughter. The novel is essentially a lengthy form of Final Words.

The examples and stories I have shared here and throughout this book serve as powerful reminders that creating a healing legacy through the written word may be a natural—perhaps even essential—part of the human spirit. As baby boomers lose parents and face their own mortality, they are recognizing a need to transcend the egocentrism that surrounded this cohort group. Creating healing legacies may meet part of that need. And it will help all of us to keep in mind that leaving such legacies does not have to be a complex ordeal. The simplest words and phrases that so often go unsaid are those that make life meaningful and help heal emotional wounds: *You were a good son . . . You were the best mother you could be . . . Thank you for all your sacrifices . . . I forgive you . . . I love you.*

The current rituals of writing a last will and testament, planning our funeral services, and writing living wills are good and important. But as we consider all of this preparation, the missing piece is obvious: none of it includes direct, personal words to our grieving loved ones or to those who may die soon. We take care of business, but we don't take care of relationships. Writing Final Words and Legacy Letters provides a way to honor relationships and facilitate the healing process.

It's a different kind of inheritance—one that can prevent us from missing the moments.

Let me close by asking one last time, If you don't write final messages to your loved ones, who will? Leave nothing unsaid.

Appendix I

ADULT SAMPLE FORMAT FOR WRITING FINAL WORDS TO AN INDIVIDUAL

Use this outline to write final messages. But before you read it, I encourage you to try writing your own words first. If you get stuck or need ideas, you can always come back later.

Final Words for_____

Today's Date _____

Dear _____,

I am writing this to you when I am _____ years old and in good health. You are _____ years old and also in good health . . . (add any other descriptors about you or the person to whom you are writing).

Possible topic sentences:
   What I admire most about you . . .
   Some of my special memories of you (or us) . . .
   Thank you for . . .
   I regret . . .
   We haven't talked much in the past few years. If I offended
      you, I am truly sorry . . .
   Though you hurt me when . . . , I want you to know that
      I forgive you . . .

Reflections on values, life messages, spiritual or religious lessons:

>   Some of the things I have learned about life and want to
>   share . . .
>   Family values I hope you will pass on . . .
>   I believe (religious thoughts) . . .

My life (moments of pride, career highlights, armed forces unit, etc.):

>   You may or may not know this but . . .

Future hopes and wishes:

>   My hopes for you include . . . (family values, life messages,
>   spiritual or religious lessons)
>   I ask that you take good care of . . . (or other special
>   requests of this person)
>   I hope you will remember me as . . .

Expression of love:

Expression of good-bye:

Handwritten signature:

Appendix II

ADULT SAMPLE FORMAT FOR WRITING FINAL WORDS TO A GROUP

Use this outline to write final messages. But before you read it, I encourage you to try writing your own words first. If you get stuck or need ideas, you can always come back later.

Final Words for_____

Today's Date _____

Dear _____,

I am writing this to you when I am _____ years old, in good health, and _____ (add any other relevant information about you or members of the group).

Possible topic sentences:
   All of you have been important to me because . . .
   Some of my special memories of us are . . .
   Thank you for . . .
   I regret . . .
   What I learned from all of you . . .
   What I have valued most from all of you . . .

Reflections on family values, life messages, spiritual or religious lessons:

    Some of the things I have learned about life and want
        to share . . .

    Family values I hope you will pass on . . .

    I believe (religious) . . .

My life (moments of pride, career highlights, armed forces unit, etc.):

    You may or may not know this but . . .

Future hopes and wishes:

    My hopes for all of you include . . . (family values, life
        messages, group vision)

    I ask that you . . . (any special requests of this group)

    I hope you will remember me as . . .

Expression of love:

Expression of good-bye:

Handwritten signature:

Appendix III

CHILD AND TEEN SAMPLE FORMAT FOR WRITING FINAL WORDS TO AN INDIVIDUAL

Before reading this, try sitting down to write your messages first. If you really don't know what to say, then please use this outline as a guide.

Final Words for_____

Today's Date _____

Dear _____,

I am writing this to you when I am _____ years old and you are _____ (add anything else to describe "you" and the person you are writing).

Possible topic sentences:
   What I admire most about you . . .
   Some of my special memories of you (or us) . . .
   Thank you for . . .
   I regret . . .
   If I ever made you mad, I am truly sorry . . .
   Though you hurt me when_____, I want you to know
      that I forgive you . . .

Reflections on what is important to you . . . your values, religious beliefs, or lessons:

 What I have learned about life is . . .

 What I value about life is . . .

 I believe (religious thoughts) . . .

My life (moments of pride, school highlights, etc.):

 Something I am really proud of is . . .

Future hopes and wishes:

 I hope that you . . .

 Please take good care of. . . .

 Remember me as . . .

Expression of love:

Expression of good-bye:

Handwritten signature:

Appendix IV

CHILD AND TEEN SAMPLE FORMAT FOR WRITING FINAL WORDS TO A GROUP

Before reading this, try sitting down to write your messages first. If you really don't know what to say, then use this outline as a guide.

Final Words for_____

Today's Date _____

Dear _____,

I am writing this to you when I am _____ years old (add any other information about you or the group of people you are writing).

Possible topic sentences:
    All of you have been important to me because . . .
    Some of my special memories are . . .
    Thank you for . . .
    I'm sorry for . . .
    I wish that . . .
    What I learned from all of you . . .
    I believe (religious thoughts) . . .

Unique parts of your life (moments of pride, school, artistic, or athletic highlights):

Special messages to individual people:
    Family members . . .
    Friends . . .
    People at school, athletic teams, or other activities . . .
    Neighbors . . .

Future hopes and wishes:
    I hope all of you . . . (special wishes or goals for this group)
    I ask that you . . . (any special requests for this group)
    I hope you will remember me as . . .

Expression of love:

Expression of good-bye:

Handwritten signature:

Appendix V

SAMPLE FORMAT FOR LEGACY LETTER OF AFFIRMATION AND FINAL GOOD-BYE

This letter is most appropriate for loved ones who are elderly, terminally ill, or going into harm's way. Suggested elements of the letter are listed below. Please add or subtract as appropriate. Before reading, try to write your own letter first and see what you have to say.

Legacy Letter for _____

Today's Date _____

Dear _____,

Introduction:

I am writing to you at this time because there are some things I want to make sure you know. It's never certain when any of us will die, and I don't want to leave anything unsaid . . .

Affirmation

Describe what you admire about this person (personal virtues or traits, life achievements at home or in career, etc.).

Gratitude

Express thanks to this person for both small and large life gifts.

Memories

Share memories . . . include happy, fun, sad (if appropriate) ones. Go as far back as you want. Describe memories between the two of you, family memories, treasured moments. Be generous. People never tire of good memories, and they can provide the comfort of a handmade quilt at the end of life.

Regrets

Identify your regrets, if any. Describe how your regrets may have affected this person and what you learned from them, or simply acknowledge the regrets and let them stand on their own.

Forgiveness: If you need to ask for or grant forgiveness, please do.

Personal legacy:

Name specific family legacies this person will leave—they can be spiritual or tangible.

Expression of love:

Expression of good-bye (if appropriate or if the loved one is terminally ill):

Handwritten signature:

NOTES

CHAPTER 1

1. Fitzgerald, Helen. "Managing Stress for Hospice Workers." American Hospice Foundation. Washington (DC): March 6, 2002. (accessed June 25, 2005). http://www.americanhospice.org/articles/hospicestress.htm.

2. Chochinov, H., Hack, T., Hassard, T., Kristjansom, L., McClement, S., and Harlos, M. (2005). "Dignity Therapy: A Novel Psychotherapeutic Intervention for Patients near the End of Life." *Journal of Clinical Oncology* 23:5520–26.

3. Anderson, M. (2004). *Sacred Dying: Creating Rituals for Embracing the End of Life.* New York: Marlowe & Company.

4. Reimer, J. (1991). *So That Your Values Live On: Ethical Wills and How to Prepare Them.* Philadelphia, PA: Jewish Lights.

5. Andreae, C. (2000). *When Evening Comes: The Education of a Hospice Volunteer.* New York: St. Martin's.

6. Fitzgerald, "Managing Stress."

7. Gill, Elizabeth (Randolph-Macon College). "Death and Dying." E-mail message to the author, August 4, 2003.

8. Cheney, K. (September/October 2004). "Gift of a Lifetime." AARP, The Magazine, 36.

9. Baines, B. (2001). *Ethical Wills: Putting Your Values on Paper.* Philadelphia, PA: Perseus Books.

10. Cheney, "Gift of a Lifetime," 36.

11. Reimer, *So That Your Values Live On.*

12. Freed, R. (2003). *Women's Lives, Women's Legacies: Passing Your Beliefs and Blessings to Future Generations: Creating Your Own Spiritual-Ethical Will.* New York: Fairview Press.

13. Ethical Will. "Ethical Wills: Preserving Your Legacy of Values." (accessed January 6, 2005). http://www.ethicalwill.com/ index.html.

14. Moldeven, Mike. Caregiver Network Inc. The Ethical Will. (accessed September 4, 2004). http://www.caregiver.ca/cgcilgew.html.

15. Norris, Michelle. "War at Home: Families Share Last Letters Home." *All Things Considered,* National Public Radio. Washington (DC): All Things Considered. November 11, 2004. (accessed June 25, 2005). http://www.npr.org/templates/story/story.php?storyId=4165188.

16. Powers, Laura. "Henry Potter's Will." Cumberland County (NC). *Cumberland County Will Book*, pg. 377 1180C. (accessed July 10, 2005) http://www.rootsweb.com/~nccumber/willindx.htm#potter.

17. Byock, I. (1997). *Dying Well: Peace and Possibilities at the End of Life.* New York: Riverhead Books, 120.

18. Hahn, T. N. (1975). *The Miracle of Mindfulness: An Introduction to the Practice of Meditation.* Boston: Beacon Press, 51.

CHAPTER 2

1. Muehler, John (Bon Secours Hospital). "Book." E-mail message to the author, June 28, 2005 (accessed July 5, 2005).

2. Gilligan, S. G. (1988). "Symptom Phenomena as Trance Phenomena." In J. Zeig and S. Lankton, eds., *Ericksonian Psychotherapy: State of the Art.* New York: Brunner Mazel.

3. Warren, R. (2002). *The Purpose Driven Life: What On Earth Am I Here For?* Grand Rapids, MI: Zondervan.

4. Ackerman, D. (2004). *An Alchemy of Mind.* New York: Scribner.

5. Johnson, R. (1993). *Owning Your Own Shadow: Understanding the Dark Side of the Psyche.* San Francisco: HarperCollins, 34.

6. Smith, H. I. (2004). *Grievers Ask: Answers to Questions about Death and Loss.* Minneapolis: Augsburg Books.

7. Kubler-Ross, E. (1969). *On Death and Dying.* New York: Macmillan.

8. James, J., and Friedman, R. (1998). *The Grief Recovery Handbook: The Action Program for Moving Beyond Death, Divorce, and Other Losses.* New York: HarperPerennial.

9. Moody, R., and Arcangel, D. (2001). *Life After Loss: Conquering Grief and Finding Hope.* San Francisco: HarperSanFrancisco.

10. Noel, B., and Blair, P. (2000). *I Wasn't Ready to Say Goodbye: Surviving, Coping, and Healing After the Sudden Death of a Loved One.* Milwaukee, WI: Champion Press.

11. Prigerson, H., and Jacobs, S. (1999). "Consensus Criteria for Traumatic Grief: A Preliminary Empirical Test." *British Journal of Psychiatry* 174:67.

12. Kaltman, S., and Bonanno, G. (2002). "Trauma and Bereavement: Examining the Impact of Sudden and Violent Deaths." *Journal of Anxiety Disorders* 17:131–47.

13. James and Friedman, *Grief Recovery Handbook.*

14. Smith, *Grievers Ask.*

15. Shannon, A. (May/June 2005). "Beloved Stranger: Temperament and the Elusive Concept of Normality." *Psychotherapy Networker* 29(3): 62–69.

16. Mayer, J. (2005). "A Tale of Two Visions: Can a New View of Personality Help Integrate Psychology?" *American Psychologist* 60:294–307.

17. Myers, I. (1995). *Gifts Differing: Understanding Personality Type.* Palo Alto, CA: Davies-Black.

18. Costa, P., and McCrae, R. (1992). *Revised NEO Personality Inventory (NEO-PI-R) and NEO Five Factor Inventory (NEO-FFI) Professional Manual.* Odessa, FL: Psychological Assessment Resources.

19. Hedtke, L., and Winslade, J. (2004). *Re-membering Lives: Conversations with the Dying and the Bereaved.* Amityville, NY: Baywood.

20. Halberstam, Y., and Leventhal, J. (1997). *Small Miracles: Extraordinary Coincidences from Everyday Life.* Holbrook, MA: Adams Media.

21. Ibid, 40–42.

CHAPTER 3

1. DeSpelder, L. A., and Strickland, A. L. (2002). *The Last Dance: Encountering Death and Dying,* 6th ed. Boston: McGraw Hill.

2. Leming, M., and Dickinson, G. (2002). *Understanding Dying, Death, and Bereavement,* 5th ed. Ft. Worth, TX: Harcourt College.

3. Kearl, M. C. (1989). *Endings: A Sociology of Death and Dying.* New York: Oxford University Press.

4. Nuland, S. (1994) *How We Die: Reflections on Life's Final Chapter.* New York: Alfred Knopf, 243.

5. Kearl, Michael. "Images across Cultures and Time." Trinity University San Antonio, TX: (accessed July 17, 2005) http://www.trinity.edu/~mkearl/death-1.html#cu.

6. Hedtke and Winslade, *Re-Membering Lives.*

7. Remembering Practices.(accessed July 12, 2005) www.rememberingpractices.com.

8. Turner, V. (1982) *From Ritual to Theatre: The Human Seriousness of Play.* New York: PAJ Publications.

9. Taylor, Richard P. (2000). *Death and the Afterlife: A Cultural Encyclopedia.* Santa Barbara, CA: ABC-CLIO.

10. Ibid.

11. Chidester, D. (1990). *Patterns of Transcendence: Religion, Death, and Dying.* Belmont, CA: Wadsworth.

12. Gamino, L. A., Easterling, L. W., Stirman, L. S., and Sewell, K. (2000). "Grief Adjustment as Influenced by Funeral Participation and Occurrence of Adverse Funeral Events." *Omega: The Journal of Death and Dying* 41(2): 79–92.

13. Taylor, *Death and the Afterlife.*

14. Ibid.

15. Aging with Dignity. (2001). *Five Wishes.* Tallahassee, FL: Aging with Dignity. www.agingwithdignity.org.

16. Hospice of Michigan (2005). (accessed July 18, 2005). http://www.hom.org/movement.asp.

17. Stoddard, S. (1978). *The Hospice Movement: A Better Way of Caring for the Dying.* New York: Vintage Books.

18. National Hospice and Palliative Care Association. Alexandria, VA: History of Hospice Care. (accessed June 1, 2005). http://www.nhpco.org/i4a/pages/index.cfm?pageid=3285.

19. Ibid.

20. O'Gorman, S. M. (1998). "Death and Dying in Contemporary Society: An Evaluation of Current Attitudes and the Rituals Associated with Death and Dying and Their Relevance to Recent Understandings of Health and Healing." *Journal of Advanced Nursing* 27(6): 1127–35.

21. Chidester, *Patterns of Transcendence.*

22. Kalish, R. (1980). *Death and Dying: Views from Many Cultures.* Farmingdale, NY: Baywood.

23. Kemp, C. (2002). "Culture and the End of Life: A Review of Major World Religions." *Journal of Hospice and Palliative Nursing* 7(4): 235–42.

24. Braun, K., and Nichols, R. (1997). "Death and Dying in Four Asian American Cultures: A Descriptive Study." *Death Studies* 21(4): 327–59.

25. Salvador, R. J. (2003). "What Do Mexicans Celebrate on the Day of the Dead?" In J. D. Morgan and P. Laungani, eds., *Death and Bereavement in the Americas,* Death, Value, and Meaning Series, Vol. 2. Amityville, NY: Baywood, 75–76

26. Kearl, *Endings.* (See ch. 3, n. 3.)

27. Munet-Vilaro, F. (1998). "Grieving and Death Rituals of Latinos." *Oncology Nursing Forum* 25(10): 1761–63.

28. Romano, Salvatore. "Italian epitaphs." E-mail message to the author. July 16, 2005.

CHAPTER 5

1. Gross, J. J. (2002). "Emotion Regulation: Affective, Cognitive, and Social Consequences." *Psychophysiology* 39(3): 281–91.

2. Powers, S., Welsh, D., and Wright, V. (1994). "Adolescents' Affective Experience of Family Behaviors: The Role of Subjective Understanding." *Journal of Research on Adolescence* 4:585–600.

3. Gross, J. J., and Levenson, R. W. (1997). "Hiding Feelings: The Acute Effects

of Inhibiting Negative and Positive Emotion." *Journal of Abnormal Psychology* 106(1): 95–103.

4. Goleman, D. 1995. *Emotional Intelligence: Why It Matters More Than IQ.* New York: Bantam.

5. Mayer, J., and Salovey, P. (1997). "What Is Emotional Intelligence?" In P. Salovey and D. Sluyter, eds., *Emotional Development and Emotional Intelligence.* New York: Basic Books.

6. Congliosi, Karen. "Healing through the Written Word. *The Permanente Journal:* Portland, OR (Summer 2002) (accessed July 19, 2005). http://xnet.kp.org/permanentejournal/sum02/healing.html.

7. Spiegel, D. (1999). "Healing Words: Emotional Expression and Disease Outcome." *Journal of the American Medical Association* 281(14): 1328–29.

8. Pennebaker, J. (1995). *Emotion, Disclosure, and Health.* Washington, DC: American Psychological Association.

9. Ibid.

10. Smyth, J. M., Stone A. A., Hurewitz, A., and Kaell, A. (1999). "Effects of Writing about Stressful Experiences on Symptom Reduction in Patients with Asthma or Rheumatoid Arthritis: A Randomized Trial." *Journal of the American Medical Association* 281(14): 1304–09.

11. Ibid.

12. Pennebaker J. (1997). *Opening Up: The Healing Power of Expressing Emotions.* New York: Guilford Press, 185.

13. Ibid.

14. DeSalvo L. (1999). *Writing as a Way of Healing: How Telling Our Stories Transforms Our Lives.* San Francisco: HarperSanFrancisco.

15. Congliosi, "Healing through the Written Word."

16. Kennedy-Morre, E., and Watson, J. C. (2001). "How and When Does Emotional Expression Help?" *Review of General Psychology* 5:187–212.

17. LePore, S., and Smyth, J. (2002). *The Writing Cure: How Expressive Writing Promotes Health and Emotional Well-Being.* Washington, DC: American Psychological Association.

18. Byock, *Dying Well.* (See Ch. 1, n. 18.)

CHAPTER 6

1. Basow, S. (1992). *Gender Stereotypes: Roles and Alternatives.* New York: Brooks/Cole.

2. Ibid.

3. Hutson-Comeaux, S., and Kelly, J. (2002). "Gender Stereotypes of Emotional Reactions: How We Judge an Emotion as Valid." *Sex Roles* 47(1–2): 1–10.

4. Anderson, B. S., and Zinsser, J. P. (1989). *A History of Their Own: Women in Europe from Prehistory to the Present.* Vol. 1. New York: Harper and Row.

5. Eisler, R. (1988). *The Chalice and the Blade: Our Past; Our Future.* New York: HarperCollins.

6. French, K. L., and Poska, A. M. (2006). *Women and Gender in the Western Past. New York: Houghton-Mifflin.*

7. De Beauvoir, S. (1952). *The Second Sex.* New York: Bantam Books.

8. Friedan, B. (1963). *The Feminine Mystique.* New York: Dell.

9. Mack-Canty, C. (2004). "Third-Wave Feminism and the Need to Reweave the Nature/Culture Duality." *NWSA Journal* 16(3): 154–79.

10. Springer, K. (2002). "Third Wave Black Feminism?" *Signs: Journal of Women in Culture and Society* 27(4): 1059–82.

11. Levant, R. F. (2001). "The Crises of Boyhood." In G. R. Brooks and G. Good, eds., *The New Handbook of Counseling and Psychotherapy for Men.* Vol. 1. San Francisco: Jossey-Bass, 424–39.

12. Tronick, E. Z., and Cohn, J. F. (1989). "Infant-Mother Face-to-Face Interaction: Age and Gender Differences in Coordination and the Occurrence of Miscoordination." *Child Development* 60(1): 85–92.

13. Polce-Lynch, M., Myers, B. J., Kilmartin, C., Forssmann-Falk, R., and Kliewer, W. (1998). "Gender and Age Patterns in Body Image, Emotional Expression and Self-Esteem: A Qualitative Analysis." *Sex Roles* 38(11–12): 1025–48.

14. Polce-Lynch, M., Myers, B. J., Kliewer, W. and Kilmartin, C. (2001). "Adolescent Self-Esteem and Gender: Exploring Relations to Sexual Harassment, Body Image, Media and Emotional Expression." *Journal of Youth and Adolescence* 30(2): 225–44.

15. Hochschild, A. (1990). *The Second Shift.* New York: Avon Books.

16. Orbuch, T., and Timmer, S. (2001). "Differences in His and Her Marriage." In D. Vannoy, ed., *Gender Mosaics: Social Perspectives.* Los Angeles: Roxbury Press, 155–64.

17. Aldous, J., Mulligan, G., and Bjarnason, T. (1998). "Fathering Over Time: What Makes the Difference?" *Journal of Marriage and Family* 60(4): 809–20.

CHAPTER 7

1. Lynch, J. R., and Kilmartin, C. T. (1999). *The Pain Behind the Mask: Overcoming Masculine Depression.* Binghamton, NY: Haworth Press.

2. Polce-Lynch, M. (2002). *Boy Talk: How You Can Help Your Son Express His Emotions.* Oakland, CA: New Harbinger.

3. Pollack, W. (1998). *Real Boys: Rescuing Our Sons from the Myths of Boyhood.* New York: Holt.

4. Lynch, J. R. (June 23, 2005). "Psychology of Men." Lecture to undergraduate class in Psychology of Gender. Randolph-Macon College, Ashland, VA.

5. United States Bureau of the Census. (1997). *Statistical Abstract of the United States* (117th edition). Washington, DC: U.S. Government Printing Office.

6. Hoyert, D, Kochanek, M. A., and Murphy, S. L. (1999). "Deaths: Final Data for 1997." *National Vital Statistics Report,* 47(19).

7. Colburn, D. (January 23, 1996). "Suicide Rate Climbs for Older Americans." *Washington Post,* Health section, WH5.

8. United States Bureau of the Census, *Statistical Abstract of the United States* (117th edition).

9. Kilmartin, C. (2000). *The Masculine Self,* 2nd ed. Boston: McGraw-Hill.

10. Courtenay, W. H. (2003). "Key Determinants of the Health and Well-Being of Men and Boys." *International Journal of Men's Health* 2(1): 1–30.

11. Gross and Levenson, "Hiding Feelings." (See ch. 5, n. 3.)

12. Gross, "Emotion Regulation." (See ch. 5, n. 1.)

13. Real, T. (1999). "Male Depression." Richmond, VA: Richmond Clinical Society of Social Work. Annual Conference.

14. Byock, *Dying Well.* (See ch. 5, n. 18)

15. LeDoux, J. (1998). *The Emotional Brain: The Mysterious Underpinnings of Emotional Life.* New York: Simon and Schuster.

16. LePore and Smyth, *Writing Cure.* (See ch. 5, n. 17.)

17. Levenson, R. W. (2000). "Expressive, Physiological, and Subjective Changes in Emotion across Adulthood." In S. H. Qualls and N. Abeles, eds., *Psychology and the Aging Revolution: How We Adapt to Longer Life.* Washington, D.C.: American Psychological Association, 123–40.

18. Pennebaker, J., *Opening Up.* (See ch. 5, n. 12.)

19. Caplan, P., and Caplan, J. (1995). *Thinking Critically about Research on Sex and Gender.* New York: HarperCollins.

20. Gur, R. C., Mozley, L. H., Mozley, P. D., Resnick, S. M., Karp, J. S., Alavi, A., Arnold, S. E., and Gur, R. E. (1995). "Sex Differences in Regional Cerebral Glucose Metabolism During a Resting State." *Science* 267(5197): 526–31.

21. Gurian, M., and Stevens, K. (2005). *The Minds of Boys: Saving Our Sons from Falling Behind in School and Life.* New York: Jossey-Bass.

22. Camras, L. A., Meng, Z., Ujiie, T., Dharamsi, S., Miyake, K., Oster, H., Wang, L., Cruz, J., Murdoch, A., and Campos, J. (2002). "Observing Emotion in Infants: Facial Expression, Body Behavior, and Rater Judgments of Eesponses to an Expectancy-Violating Event." *Emotion* 2(2): 179–93.

23. Tronick and Cohn, "Infant-Mother Face-to-Face Interaction." (See ch. 6, n. 12.)

24. Levant, "Crises of Boyhood." (See ch. 6, n. 11)

25. Polce-Lynch, Myers, et al. "Gender and Age Patterns in Body Image." (See ch. 6, n. 13.)

26. Polce-Lynch, Myers, et al. "Adolescent Self-Esteem and Gender." (See ch. 6, n. 14.)

CHAPTER 8

1. Grollman, E. A. (1990). *Talking about Death.* Boston: Beacon Press.

2. Kroen, W. (1999). *Helping Children Cope with the Loss of a Loved One: A Guide for Grown-Ups.* Minneapolis, MN: Free Spirit.

3. Worden, J. W. (2001). *Children and Grief: When a Parent Dies.* New York: Guilford Press.

4. Shaffer, D. (2001). *Developmental Psychology: Childhood and Adolescence,* 6th ed. New York: Wadsworth.

5. Polce-Lynch, *Boy Talk.* (See ch. 7, n. 2.)

6. Greenspan, S. 1993. *Playground Politics: Understanding the Emotional Life of Your School Age Child.* Reading, MA: Addison Wesley Longman.

7. Piaget, J. (1952). *The Origins of Intelligence in Children.* New York: International University Press.

8. Corr, C., and Corr, D., eds. (1996). *Handbook of Childhood Death and Bereavement.* New York: Springer.

9. Harter, S., and Whitesell, N. (1989). "Developmental Changes in Children's Understanding of Single, Multiple, and Blended Emotion Concepts." In C. Saarnin and P. Harris, eds., *Children's Understanding of Emotion.* New York: Cambridge University Press.

10. Giedd, J. N., Snell, J. W., Lange, N., Rajapakse, J. C., Casey, B. J., Kozuch, P. L., Vaituzis, A. C., Vauss, Y. C., Hamburger, S. D., Kaysen, D,. and Rapoport, J. L. (1996). "Quantitative Magnetic Resonance Imaging of Human Brain Development: Ages 4–18." *Cerebral Cortex* 6(4): 551–60.

11. Harris, P. L., and Giménez, M. H. (2005). "Children's Acceptance of Conflicting Testimony: The Case of Death." *Journal of Cognition and Culture* 5(1–2): 143–64.

12. Corr, C. and Balk, D., eds. (1996). *Handbook of Adolescent Death and Bereavement.* New York: Springer.

13. Spinks, Sarah. "Adolescent Brains Are Works in Progress: Here's Why." *Frontline,* PBS. (Accessed Julyn 23, 2005) Http://www.pbs.org/ wgbh/pages/ frontline/shows/teenbrain/work/adolescent.html.

14. Corr and Balk, *Handbook of Adolescent Death and Bereavement.*

15. Kreicbergs, U., Valdimarsdóttir, U., Onelöv, E., Henter, J., and Steineck, G. (2004). "Talking about Death with Children Who Have Severe Malignant Disease." *New England Journal of Medicine* 351(12): 1175–86.

16. Sheehy, G. (1977). *Passages: Predictable Crises of Adult Life*. New York: Bantam.

CHAPTER 9

1. Callanan, M., and Kelley, P. (1992). *Final Gifts: Understanding the Special Awareness, Needs, and Communications of the Dying*. New York: Bantam, 159.

2. Tyrangiel, J. (October 3, 2005). "The Resurrection of Neil Young." *Time*.

3. Enright, R., and North, J., eds. (1998). *Exploring Forgiveness*. Madison: University of Wisconsin Press.

4. Worthington, E. (2003). *Forgiving and Reconciling: Bridges to Wholeness and Hope*. Downer's Grove, IL: InterVarsity Press.

5. Mother Teresa (1996). *A Gift for God: Prayers and Meditations*. Reprint ed. San Francisco: HarperSanFrancisco, 12.

6. Wescott, C. G. (June 2005). Father and Son. *Reader's Digest*, 112–19.

7. Coetzee, J. M. (1998). *Age of Iron*. New York: Penguin.

Acknowledgments

MANY PEOPLE HELPED the idea of healing legacies become the book you are holding in your hands. Kathryn Lynch, my step-daughter, launched the project by carefully editing the proposal. Susan Schulman, my literary agent, found the right publisher in Marlowe & Company where Matthew Lore has developed an excellent line of books on death education. And Renee Sedliar's editing team polished the final manuscript in a way that only good editors can.

Maggie Callanan and Patricia Kelley's hospice research served as a catalyst in the early stages of this project. Ira Byock's leadership in living and dying well provided information and inspiration, as did James Pennebaker's pioneering research with emotional expression. I also thank them for their support of this book.

Each time I spoke with someone about creating a ritual for final messages, their enthusiasm and feedback shaped the book in valuable ways. Some of these people include Cathy Cawley, Kim Forbes, Joe Bauserman, Chris Kilmartin, Mary Leffler, Vic Malloy and the VIP Care Staff, John Muehler, and Carol and Michael Daily. I thank Beth Gill and Jordan Kilgour at Randolph-Macon College for helpful discussions, along with many other colleagues and students.

I am very grateful to several people who shared important stories, bringing this book to life in a real way: Elsie Cimorelli, Meg Pienkowski, and Margaret Flowers and her family.

Rachel and Morgan Lynch, my daughters, liked the idea of Final Words and Legacy Letters from the start. They graciously made room for the book as if it were a new sibling. But their cooperation was not without cost. I wasn't as available as they needed me to be this past year because I was often writing. I thank them for their maturity and support. John Lynch, my husband, carried my half of the sky at home without complaint and gave the gift of endless writing hours. But there was a cost to him as well. Writing absorbed my attention and deadlines often preempted plans, like the time climbing Old Rag mountain turned into a walk around the block. A psychologist and author himself, John not only understood, he also provided critical feedback and excellent ideas. I thank him for his constant generosity and grace.

I have had an inner passion about the idea of writing final messages. Whom do I acknowledge? I don't know for sure, but I suspect it is the source of all that is good. For me, this is God. I shared my own faith and included different religions in this book as an intentional way to encourage inter-religious dialogue about life, death, and healing. History and current world events continue to reveal a need for understanding one another's faith traditions.

This book grew out of a personal family story so I must finally acknowledge my mother, Esther Polce, for her trust and courage. This book would not exist without her.